Praise for BOMBAY TO BREW CITY

Bombay to Brew City: Reflections of a Cheesehead from India, is an entertaining new memoir from Dr. Balaraman Kalyanaraman. Dr. Kalyanaraman is an internationally renowned scientist and expert on using electron paramagnetic resonance (EPR) to address problems in free radical biology. A seemingly esoteric area, his work has had a profound impact on areas as diverse as Parkinson's disease and cancer. In this short and deeply personal account, he reflects on his life, his formative career experiences, and his and others' important contributions to science. In nine compact chapters, he recounts his intellectual and personal journey from a small town in India to the US South, and ultimately to Milwaukee, Wisconsin.

Each chapter is peppered with disparate, interesting, and humorous observations; little-known facts both scientific and otherwise; and insights and reflections on his own thoughts as he developed into a world-class scientist. Along the way, he shares with us not only his scientific achievements but also formative personal adventures. Dr. Kalyanaraman writes with humor while relating his wonder for a new culture, and his gratitude for the good fortune of friends and mentors that supported him and helped him succeed.

This memoir is ultimately a testament to a life in science as a journey of both scientific and personal growth, and how the two are inextricably linked. It will be of particular interest to those who are on their own journey in science, especially those who are pursuing their passion in a new land. At the end of this account, they will find they have met a fellow traveler who has pioneered the path. Much will resonate for those who have also been down that road and for younger scientists as they pursue their journey across cultures, and Dr. Kalyanaraman's account may give some new insights into this journey for those who haven't.

—Ravi Misra, PhD
Associate Provost, Accreditation and Program Development;
Dean, School of Graduate Studies, Medical College of Wisconsin

"Go west, young man. Go west," were Horace Greeley's famous words to those who sought to improve their place in life. In the case of Balaraman Kalyanaraman, "Go west," meant an 8,500-mile trek from the streets of Madras to research laboratories in Milwaukee. Dr. Kalyanaraman's memoir, *Bombay to Brew City: Reflections of a Cheesehead from India*, is the inspiring story of a boy from a southeast Indian metropolis who became a distinguished scientist, whose groundbreaking research is expanding our understanding of cancer and Parkinson's disease. It's the story of blended cultures in which a young man expands his love for cricket to American football. Through Dr. Kalyanaraman's eyes, we see the potential that exists in each of the eight billion individuals who walk this planet.

—Richard Katschke
Chief Historian, Medical College of Wisconsin

BOMBAY TO BREW CITY

Reflections of a Cheesehead from India

BALARAMAN KALYANARAMAN, PHD

www.ten16press.com - Waukesha, WI

Bombay to Brew City: Reflections of a Cheesehead from India

ISBN PB: 9781645384977
ISBN HC: 9781645384960

Bombay to Brew City: Reflections of a Cheesehead from India
by Balaraman Kalyanaraman

For information, please contact:

www.ten16press.com
Waukesha, WI

Editor: Jenna Bruemmer
Cover Designer: Kaeley Dunteman
Cover Images Credit: Regina Simonsen

I DEDICATE THIS BOOK TO:

my parents, wife, children,
granddaughter, family, and friends.
My accomplishments would not have
been possible without their love
and encouragement.

CONTENTS

PREFACE

"Ideas don't come out fully formed. They only become clear as you work on them. You just have to get started."
—Mark Zuckerberg

Each of us has a story to tell. And every immigrant has a story to tell. With nearly eight billion people in the world, all our stories are unique, and all of our journeys have taken different paths; that is the beauty of our upbringings in different parts of the globe with diverse cultures. Every human being is dealt a different hand of cards: Some are born with a silver spoon in their mouth, and some with no spoon at all. Some have extraordinary skills in athletics or public speaking, and some struggle to walk or talk. Fortunately, I have lived a blessed life.

I grew up in Chennai (formerly named Madras), a metropolitan city with several million people in the state of Tamil Nadu in South India. After finishing my high school and undergraduate education, I moved to a much larger city, Mumbai (formerly named Bombay), located in the western part of India, where I earned my master's degree and then worked for a year at a pharmaceutical company. I was restless and bored with the monotony of the work; I needed to make a change, so I came to the United States for my doctoral studies. My first stop was El Paso, Texas. Following my first (and only) semester at the University of Texas at El Paso, I was offered a research fellowship for a PhD in chemistry at the University of Alabama in Tuscaloosa—one of the key turning points in my life. Upon receiving my PhD, I began a three-year postdoctoral training at the National Institute of Environmental Health Sciences in Research Triangle Park, North Carolina, and lived in an apartment complex near Chapel Hill—another huge turning point! During that time, I met the love of my life: a wonderful young woman named Lilian. A year later, after Lilian graduated from college, we got married and moved to Milwaukee, Wisconsin. I began a second postdoctoral training, this time at the Medical College of Wisconsin, and Lilian began working as a tax specialist. In the forty years that followed, I rose through the ranks from postdoctoral fellow to department chair. Over the years, my research has focused on understanding the biological, physiological, and toxicological significance of free radicals generated from oxygen and environmental chemicals, and the role of mitochondria—the cell powerhouse generating energy—in cancer and neurodegenerative disorders. My research group and I have developed new molecules that can be converted to drugs for treating diseases, particularly Parkinson's and cancer. We have received US, European, and international patents for some of these molecules. Scientifically, I am in the top 1% most-cited authors in the world in the fields of biochemistry and molecular biology, oncology and carcinogenesis, and biomedical research (Baas, Boyack, and Ioannidis 2021). Ideas generated based on my strengths have been the foundation for my success. I was able to achieve success, and I believe it is possible for everyone.

Bombay to Brew City: Reflections of a Cheesehead from India describes my upbringing, schooling, and nearly fifty years of life experience in America, one of the most tolerant countries in the world, and one with unlimited opportunities. I hope you enjoy reading about the events and people that have shaped my life, and a smorgasbord of my views on growing up in India, coming to America, becoming a football fan (particularly the Alabama Crimson Tide and Green Bay Packers), working in biomedical research (including cancer and Parkinson's and other neurological diseases), philosophy, race relations, exercise, and nutrition, as well as some life lessons. At times, I have asked myself: "If I knew then what I know now, would I have done things differently?" The answer has always been, "No way, Jose." You only go through this life once, so you must make the best out of it! If you believe in the Hindu religion, and (1) do a reasonably good job with your present life, and (2) have not taken advantage of people, you might even be reincarnated and get another chance!

Why did I write this memoir? And why now? Who is going to read it? These are good questions! People all over the world, and from all walks of life, contemplate their purpose; some of them have great ideas but don't know whether to act on them or how to take them to the next level. I wrote this book with the hope that my story may lift such people up and help them realize their own potential. (Also, I figured now was a good time to write a book, as my neurons are still intact and firing reasonably well.) I started out in my research career fearing failure, rejection, embarrassment, and so forth; but mainly, I worried that my research was not creative. Later, I realized that by focusing on, and building ideas around, my own strengths, I was able to overcome my "creative fear" and achieve my personal best. This sounds simple, but too often, we focus on our weaknesses; doing this raises self-doubts, fears, and negative thoughts. If we nurture ourselves, grow, and act on those ideas based on our strengths, we will achieve *our personal best*. That, in my opinion, should be considered as success.

Chapter 1
GROWING UP IN MADRAS

"The city is full of terrible actors. That is what historians never say about Madras, it is filled with hams."
—Manu Joseph

Chennai, formerly known as Madras, is located on the coast of the Bay of Bengal and is the capital city of the state of Tamil Nadu in South India.

The population of Chennai was approximately 1.49 million in 1950, and by 2021, the population had grown to nearly 11.5 million. Chennai is nicknamed the "Detroit of India" because of the presence of major automobile makers (Ford, Hyundai, Nissan, Renault, Datsun), and tire and other automobile components manufacturers. Jayaram Jayalalithaa, a six-time chief minister of Tamil Nadu, presumably played a major role in creating this vision. Tamil is the most widely spoken language in Chennai. Next to Sanskrit, Tamil is one of the oldest languages in the world (5,000 years old) and is spoken in India, Sri Lanka, Singapore, and Malaysia. India has some thirty officially recognized languages, and each state has a different language. For example, the official language in Bengaluru (formerly known as Bangalore) in the Karnataka state is Kannada. However, the official languages of India are Hindi and English. Some of you may remember the “bleeding Madras” shirts that were popular in the 1960s. Bleeding Madras is a hand-spun yarn, and the dyes used are not colorfast. As a result, the color fades, giving the fabric a different look after every wash. These shirts were marketed in California as guaranteed to fade.

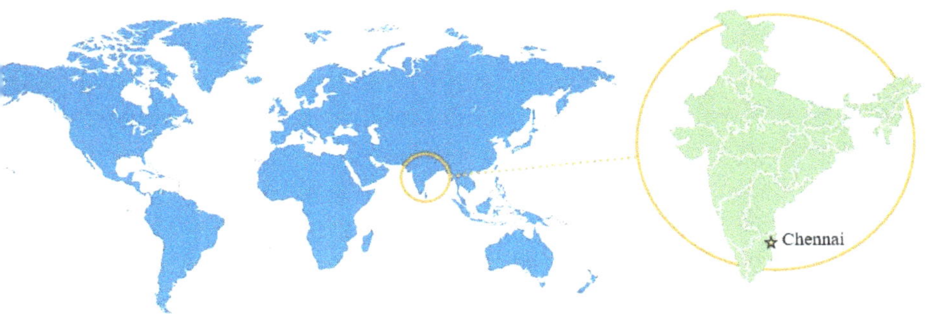

Location of Chennai, India. Map images courtesy of Freepix.com.

An actor often is referred to as a “ham.” I don’t know the origin of the word “ham,” but it refers to someone who wants to draw attention to themselves by being overly dramatic. Perhaps it was derived from the Shakespeare’s play *Hamlet*. Chennai is, and has been, the movie capital of South India. At least five Tamil Nadu chief ministers had connections to the film industry. Both Maruthur Gopala Ramachandran (M. G. R.) and Jayalalithaa (affectionately known as *Amma*, which means “mother”) were involved in writing, screenplays, and acting. While growing up, I saw many movies in which both M. G. R. and Jayalalithaa were paired in action-packed blockbusters. Arnold Schwarzenegger, the “last action hero” and former governor of California, visited Chennai and the movie studios to discuss with movie director Shankar a role in the action thriller, *I*, one of the highest-grossing Tamil films.

Schwarzenegger also met with Jayalalithaa, who then was chief minister. M. G. R. and Jayalalithaa were among the most revered and popular chief ministers of Tamil Nadu.

My grandmother came to Madras after her husband—my grandfather—died. She moved from the village of Cuddalore, which has since become a sprawling metropolis, fifty miles from Madras. At the time, my grandmother had three boys: my father, his elder brother, and his younger brother. In those days, a woman's social status was dramatically downgraded once she was widowed; she became a *persona non grata*. Unfortunately, this situation persists, to some extent, today. Rather than facing any kind of societal shunning after my grandfather's death, my grandmother took the bold step of relocating to find a better life for her sons.

Once in Madras, my grandmother worked as a cook in the house of a *zamindar* (a wealthy family who owned land) and lived in a small building near the *zamindar's* house called an outhouse, as the British named it; this building is different from the outhouse as we know it in the United States. My grandmother made sure that her sons were treated as part of the *zamindar's* family. My uncles found jobs, and my father was sent to college; he later found a job as an accountant. Both of my uncles and my father eventually got married.

My grandmother saved enough money and bought a house in Mylapore, one of the oldest suburbs of Madras.

She knew that with varying amounts of income for her sons, there had to be a long-term strategy to support the three families. She collected money from all her sons each month, depending on their incomes, to run the household and support the extended family.

The Hindu joint family structure was very common at that time in India, and my grandmother was the head of our joint family. In 2011, on a trip to India, I went to see the house. Al-

Me on the street where I grew up in Mylapore, 2011 *(left)*. Another view of the street where I grew up, 2011 *(right)*. Photo credit: Muralidharan Kazhiur.

though the original house had been remodeled, the street looked the same.

We all lived under one roof, except for my parents. My father's employer transferred him from Madras to Bombay (now named Mumbai), so they moved there. We stayed with my grandmother, as my father believed my siblings and I would benefit from the support network of our extended family. On any given day, our joint family consisted of fifteen people: One grandmother, two uncles, two aunts, seven cousins, my brother, my sister, and me. Typically, about ten of us would sit on the floor, five on each side of the room) during dinner, which was always served before 7:00 in the evening; my aunts served the food and were closely watched by my grandmother, who had to make sure there was enough food for everyone. We had no refrigerator, so food was made fresh for every meal, and only a few items kept at the warm room temperature.

At night, we slept on the floor next to each other. Each of us had a reserved spot, mat, and pillow. I did not have any difficulty falling and staying asleep for eight hours. Before 6:00 a.m. each morning, my grandmother would wake us. There was no snooze button. Her voice would be louder the second time, and that was all it took.

With fifteen or so people in one house with one bathroom and one rest room, waking promptly was a necessity. Life begins very early in the morning in India; by 6:00 a.m., the noise level of the ecosystem would be high, both inside and outside the house. I remember drinking Horlicks or Ovaltine (a British/Indian beverage) prepared by my grandmother or aunts. After age twelve, we were allowed to drink coffee, but only after we brushed our teeth. The first thing my grandmother would ask in the morning: *Did you brush your teeth?* We used toothpaste and a toothbrush only after becoming teenagers. Before then, we brushed our teeth using our index fingers and some tooth powder. I have no idea if the tooth powder contained fluoride. If it tasted sweet, it was okay with me. We did not worry about gingivitis or gum disease.

As an adult, I pondered whether one should brush their teeth before or after breakfast. Evidently, the American Dental Association has weighed in on this. I did not expect to find an elaborate discussion on this subject. Boy, was I in for a surprise, as this was one of the questions most frequently answered by the ADA. If one is planning to eat or drink something acidic, such as orange juice or coffee, it is better to brush before breakfast because acid attacks your teeth, weakening the tooth enamel. It takes thirty to forty-five minutes for saliva to restore the enamel through remineralization and brushing too soon can damage the teeth while the enamel is weakened. Just swishing with water is proposed as an alternate method to wash away acids. However, if your breakfast consists of sugary foods and drinks, then brushing after breakfast can help reduce bacteria in your mouth and prevent tooth decay. Well, there you have it—some sort of scientific explanation about brushing your teeth in the morning.

At the beginning of each summer, my grandmother would give each of us a physical exam, so to speak. If we were not gaining weight, she would say that the "damn worms" in our stomachs were eating her food. Her solution was to give us a medicine to kill the worms and then castor oil the next morning at five o'clock to poop out the worms. Some of the worms were long and scary. This may gross you out, or even freak you out, but tapeworm infections are still common in India and many other countries. A tapeworm is a parasite that, once inside the body, will live in the small intestine and feed off the food that the person is eating and digesting. If left untreated, a tapeworm can grow inside the body for years. A case study was reported in the *New England Journal of Medicine* in which a tapeworm measuring over six feet in length was extracted through a patient's mouth (Philips and Sahney 2017). The longest tapeworm ever removed was from a patient in India (who had complained for months of severe abdominal pain) and was over eighty feet (Health Facts 2018). My grandmother was way too smart for tapeworms.

Guinea worm disease is another parasitic infection that was common in many countries when I was young. It was a painful and disfiguring disease that mostly affected kids. Thanks to efforts like former President Jimmy Carter's Guinea Worm Eradication Program, the disease has been largely eradicated; the number of cases declined from 3.5 million in the mid-1980s to twenty-seven cases in 2020 (Centers for Disease Control and Prevention 2021, World Health Organization 2022). Enough said! Let me move on to cricket (the sport, not the insect), as I have spent many of my adult years talking about this game. Most Americans think a cricket match lasts longer than an Indian wedding. Robin Williams, arguably the greatest comedian, described cricket as "baseball on Valium." Cricket is wildly popular in India, and I am a huge fan. Growing up, I played the game, although not very well. As a teenager, I liked to put teams together and organize local cricket matches. My friends and I played Sundays, holidays, and after school. We spent countless hours standing at street corners in the neighborhood strategizing before the match, then discussing the highlights and lowlights after the game. With the expansion of the British Empire in the 1700s, cricket was introduced to their colonized countries, including India, Australia, New Zealand, South Africa, West Indies, Sri Lanka, and Pakistan, to name a few. Noel Coward's lyrics, "only mad dogs and Englishmen go out in the midday sun," is believed to be inspired by a phrase penned by Rudyard Kipling in his novel, *Kim*. Apparently, "Englishmen detest a siesta" (another line from Coward's song, "Mad Dogs and Englishmen"); however, they detest even more playing test matches in India during summer.

Lagaan is a term that means agricultural tax. The movie *Lagaan (*or *Lagaan: Once Upon a Time in India*, as it was named for international release), is set in 1890 when India was under British rule and each region of India was under the command of a different British officer—the famous divide and rule paradigm. In this film, Captain Russell, who is the commander of an agricultural village in central India, increased the land tax to be paid by the villagers. A young, rebellious farmer named Bhuvan is opposed to the tax increase and encourages the villagers to refuse to pay. Captain Russell, who is a cricket fanatic, proposes that he will waive the tax increase if the villagers can beat his team in a cricket match. Of course, Bhuvan and the villagers did not yet know the difference between a bat and bat crap! This movie was scored by the one and only A.R. Rahman of *Slumdog Millionaire*, so you will enjoy the dance and music, and the rest of the story. If you don't know much about cricket, I encourage you to Google it. Incidentally, Sundar Pichai, who was born in Tamil Nadu and is the CEO of Google, is a mega fan of cricket; he attended the Cricket World Cup 2019 in England.

Growing up, I was a big fan of English county cricket and players like Colin Cowdrey, Ted Dexter, Ken Barrington, Freddie

Trueman, and Geoff Boycott, to name a few. I even supported England when they played against India. We did not have a TV, but we did have a radio in our house, so I depended on the radio broadcast of the game. Owning a radio was a luxury. However, ours was not a shortwave radio, so we could not pick up the BBC. One of our affluent neighbors had a shortwave radio and usually invited guests to his house to listen to the cricket matches played in England and overseas. We would walk over to our neighbor's house, stand next to the window, and listen to BBC commentary by Brian Johnston, John Arlott, and the like. These commentators were succinct, describing the events in only a few words. Sometimes they would get into trouble for being too brief. Apparently, during a match between the West Indies and England at The Oval cricket ground in 1976, Johnston was welcoming new listeners and explaining what was happening in the game. The West Indies fast bowler Michael Holding was bowling to the opening batsman Peter Willey of England. But all that Johnston said was, "Welcome to The Oval where the bowler's Holding; the batsman's Willey." The accuracy of this quote is debated.

After I left India, I became an ardent fan of Indian cricket. India won the Cricket World Cup twice, first in 1983. On June 25, 1983, India beat the two-time world champion, the West Indies, on the Lord's cricket ground; the good Lord was on India's side. The movie *83* describes India's 1983 World Cup victory. Cricket in India is an approximately US$5 billion business. Vinod Kohli, international cricket player and former captain of India's cricket team, made the Forbes list of top 100 highest-paid athletes in 2020; he's the only cricket player to have made this list. There are about 2.5 billion followers of cricket worldwide. Next to football, or "fútbol" (soccer), cricket is the most popular game in the world.

Although my cousins, siblings, and I were in different grades, my grandmother knew when each of us had to take exams at the end of the school year and made sure we showed her our report cards. If she was not happy with our grades, we would not hear the end of it. She never bothered me, as I had decent grades in math and science; for some reason, she did not care about the other subjects. We lived near two very good high schools (grades six through twelve), so we walked to school. The medium of instruction was Tamil, except for the English class. The teachers, especially for math and science, were excellent. Even though the science books were written in Tamil, most of the teachers emphasized the importance of knowing the corresponding English words for scientific terms. It became clear to us that we would need to read science textbooks in English if we wanted to get ahead in that subject. Overall, I found the science and math classes to be engaging and enjoyable.

My grandmother was religious but not overly so. She would take me to Kapalee (Kapaleeshwarar) Temple (dedicated to Lord Shiva) once a week and before important exams at school. Prior to entering the temple, we had to remove our slippers or sandals and leave them outside; someone would take care of them for less than a penny

Usually, it would take thirty to sixty minutes to go through the *pooja* (worship rituals) once inside the temple, depending

Kapaleeshwarar Temple, 2022. Photo credit: Anuradha Cunnigaipur Dhanasekaran.

on the number of worshippers. Some days, hundreds of people would be inside the temple, and it would take the priest a lot longer to finish the *pooja*. I would tell my grandmother that everyone inside the temple was probably worrying about the sandals they left outside, while the guy outside taking care of sandals was thinking about what was going on inside the temple. That would bring a rare smile to her face.

Who would achieve *moksha* (liberation or nirvana)—the worshippers inside the temple worrying about their sandals or

Kapaleeshwarar Temple, 2022. Photo credit: Muralidharan Kazhiur.

other worldly possessions, or the sandal keeper outside the temple who was thinking about the priest and the *pooja* inside the temple? God only knows!

Chennai is known for its historical temples built in the seventh century by Cholas and Pallavas rulers. Kapalee Temple is one of the oldest temples in Tamil Nadu. There are different temples for different Hindu gods, three of them being Brahma (the Creator), Vishnu (the Protector), and Shiva (the Destroyer of Evil). In addition, there are avatars of these gods. In Sanskrit, an *avatar* is the incarnation of a Hindu deity or a god appearing on earth in bodily form (Vishnu, for example, in human or animal form). Rama was an avatar of Vishnu, and there are many Rama temples. Thanks to James Cameron, the Canadian filmmaker who popularized the word "avatar" in his blockbuster movie *Avatar*, the term is widely thought to be a genetically engineered human/*Na'vi*-hybrid body.

Long hair was taboo when I was young. My grandmother made sure that we all had a summer haircut. She would walk me to the nearby barber shop and wait outside. The barber knew that if he did not do a good job, he was in trouble, as my grandmother would not pay him until she was satisfied with the summer haircut. As I got older, my grandmother did not accompany me to the barber shop. I convinced the barber (who became my friend) not to take off too much hair. Of course, my grandmother would get mad, but slowly she gave up that fight.

My parents lived in Chembur, a suburb of Bombay. During summer vacation, my sister, my brother, and I would visit them for a couple of months. There, we could do a lot of things that weren't allowed at my grandmother's house: sleep late, eat late, go to movies, etc. After summer vacation, we would return to Madras. I got the feeling that my father was happy for us to return to Madras and continue with our routines. However, my mother seemed sad when we left.

I don't think my father ever enjoyed living in the moment. He was a worrier. He worried about the future and was constantly concerned about his health. He only slept a couple hours at night. My father suffered from headaches, migraines, and backaches; every day, he would tell us about his health issues, but we did not take him seriously. He would self-medicate to the point that some of those drugs would no longer work. Many drugs that require prescriptions in the United States are available over the counter in India; we'd ask him not to take too many of those medications. My father was kind and mild mannered, and my mother would say he was meek and lacked courage. I got along well with him. My father did nice things for others. He liked sports and listening to cricket, tennis, field hockey, and football (soccer). He did not know how to fix anything, and my mother was not happy about that. He was predictable and rarely lost his temper. I never argued with him. My father believed in going to work on time, working late, and loyalty to the workplace. That is all he knew, and he did that working as an accountant in the same company (called George Oakes, a distributor of Ford automobiles in India) for nearly four decades.

My father bought a small house in the Mylapore neighborhood of Madras, closer to my grandmother's house, in the hope that he and my mother would move there after he retired. He rented the house to a family with two kids. After a few months, the family could not afford to pay the rent. Because they had kids, my father did not want to evict them; instead, he let them stay in the house until the father found another job. After nearly a year, it became obvious that my father had been taken advantage of, and after spending a sizable amount in legal fees, that family was evicted. Thinking it was a bad omen to live in that house, my father sold it for considerably less money than it was worth.

The rental situation was different in Bombay. In the 1950s, my father rented a house under the *pagdi* rent system. In this legal tenancy system, the tenant is part owner of the rental property but not the land. Rather than paying a security deposit, the tenant pays the landlord a large percentage of the market price (referred to as the *pagdi*), and then a nominal monthly rent with minimal increases in the subsequent years; this ensures the rent does not skyrocket. Also, if a tenant has been paying the rent on time and does not cause any problems, the tenant is entitled to stay in the same place while paying the same rent; the landlord cannot sell the property as long as the tenant remains in the house. In order to get a higher rent from new tenants or sell the house for its market value, the landlord must give a large percentage of the money to the tenant(s), so they voluntarily vacate the place. Legally, it would have been nearly impossible to evict a rent-paying tenant. When vacating a property, the tenant—as part owner—usually receives a payment. Thus, when my parents decided to move from Bombay to Madras after some forty years in the same rental house, they were owed a lot of money according to the *pagdi* rental system. However, my father felt it was unethical for him to take the money because it was not his house. Everyone was flabbergasted when they learned that my parents had vacated the house without getting any *pagdi* from the landlord. Apparently, even the landlord wanted to pay some money. At that time, I did not quite appreciate my father's ethics and integrity, but now I am glad that some of those principles have slightly rubbed off on me!

My mother spent most of her time alone and was often angry with my father. She resented the fact that we were brought up by my grandmother and that we spent only a few months with her each year. She disliked the way my father used snuff and messed up his clean shirts, or when he wore wrinkled shirts to work or other places. Unfortunately, my father did not pay much attention to such details. My mother would give him the silent treatment and would not speak for days; she became moody. My relationship with her was good sometimes and strained at other times. I wish I had been more empathetic.

My cousins, aunts, and uncles were a huge part of my life in Madras, but I did not realize it at that time. My "cousin sisters," as they were called, were all nice to me and interested in what I had to say, and they would help me out. For example, one of my uncles got a phone because of his work needs. In the 1960s, not many households had phones, so it was a big deal to own one. My uncle received a few calls from his employer, and I started getting a lot of calls, as some of my friends had phones; our phone was ringing all the time. My grandmother wanted to get rid of the phone, claiming that we were charged more every time it rang. Fortunately, a few of my cousins would answer the phone, take messages, and let me know who called. My grandmother resented the fact that my cousins were covering for me. She would tell me that I should take the phone with me, and that my cousins were not my servants. Little did she know that by the 2000s, the mobile phone would transform the world, and soon after could be used to do everything from take high-resolution photos to conduct bank transactions.

My elementary/secondary school friends from the late 1950s and early 1960s have become my WhatsApp friends. We still reminisce about the times we would walk to Santhome Beach in Mylapore and sit on the sand, talking for hours. To get there, we would walk past San Thome Church. Little did I know that the church is iconic, also known as St. Thomas Cathedral Basilica, named after Saint Thomas, one of the apostles of Jesus, who brought Christianity to India as early as AD 52. San Thome Church was built by the Portuguese over the tomb of Saint Thomas nearly 500 years ago. This church is one of the three known churches in the world built over the tomb of an apostle of Jesus.

I attended Loyola College, a private Catholic higher education institution affiliated with the University of Madras. To get there from my house, I first had to take a bus, which took anywhere between twenty and forty minutes depending on traffic, and then I had to walk about one-half mile. I was invariably late getting to my first class at nine in the morning. Getting a late slip meant paying a fine at the end of each semester in addition to paying a hefty tuition. Loyola College, established in 1925 and founded by Rev. Fr. Francis Bertram, is a beautiful institution. There was a fine building called Bertram Hall. I am sure alumni such as myself, who paid many fines for being tardy and missing classes, contributed a lot to the upkeep and maintenance of that building. While at Loyola, I majored in chemistry, and had very good professors and lecturers. I am grateful for their teachings. Although I did not develop any aptitude for research there, I memorized a whole lot of organic/physical/inorganic chemistry. I obtained my bachelor's degree in 1970.

The joint family structure slowly disintegrated as my grandmother's health began to fail. Because she was bedridden with complications from diabetes, my aunts cared for her and the household. We were all getting older. My sister and cousins got married and moved away. After finishing my bachelor's degree, I decided to go to Bombay to get my master's degree in chemistry from the Indian Institute of Technology.

Before I left Madras, and before my grandmother passed away, I wish I had told her, as well as my aunts and uncles, how grateful and indebted to them I was for the love, care, and affection given to me. Not having expressed this to them is one of my biggest regrets.

Chapter 2
PURSUING ACADEMICS AND INDUSTRY IN BOMBAY

"More dreams are realized and extinguished in Bombay than any other place in India."
—Gregory David Roberts

Mumbai, which was called Bombay when I was growing up, is the gateway to India[1] and, as of 2022, the world's fourth most populous metropolis. It is both the financial capital of, and richest city in, India with the highest gross domestic product, and it is one of the most powerful and dynamic economic engines in India and around the world. Mumbai is a city of contrasts: Mukesh Ambani, an Indian billionaire businessman, and the chair and largest shareholder of Reliance Industries Ltd., resides in Mumbai, and is the tenth richest man in the world, with a net worth of

1) Mumbai is home to the Gateway of India, an arch monument that was built in the early twentieth century in commemoration of the arrival of King George V and Queen Mary at Apollo Bunder in India. The monument is one of Mumbai's top tourist attractions and is sometimes referred to as the Taj Mahal of Mumbai.

approximately US$91 billion (Forbes 2022). On the other side of the coin, more than 50% of Mumbai's population lives in slums. Mumbai is very densely populated and has more slums than any other Indian city. It is home to the Bollywood film industry, and the 2008 box office hit *Slumdog Millionaire* was filmed there. Bombay's population grew from 6.7 million in 1971 to over 20.9 million in 2022 (World Population Review).

After leaving Madras in 1970, I joined the master's degree program in chemistry at the Indian Institute of Technology (IIT) in Bombay. IITs are public institutions for higher education in science, engineering, and technology that are funded by the Indian Central Government.

Admission to the Institute is based on entrance exams performance. IITs are among the few educational institutions in India where admission is totally "cronyism free." For instance, politicians have no influence on admissions into IITs. In the 1970s, India's five IITs were in Delhi, Madras, Kanpur, Kharagpur, and Bombay. Now there are twenty-three IITs throughout India. Established in 1958, IIT Bombay retained its original name after the city name was changed to Mumbai.

IIT Bombay, located in a northern suburb of Bombay called Powai, is a city in and of itself. Only undergraduate, graduate, and postgraduate students; professors and their families; and staff are allowed to enter the campus. Students live in hostels, or dorms, professors in faculty housing, and others in staff housing. The campus contains dining halls, movie theaters, grocery stores, a gymnasium, basketball courts and soccer fields, tennis courts, and other amenities. Classes and labs were held Monday through Friday, with Saturday and Sunday off. I stayed at the postgraduate hostel.

My class comprised about twenty students from all over India. Everyone was highly motivated. We had quizzes and exams throughout the semester, so we had to study constantly.

My biggest weakness was not taking good notes during class. Since most of the test questions came from what the professors covered in class, I had to beg to borrow notes from other dedicated students, which was not always easy. After the first semester, I began to lose my motivation.

Once or twice a month, I visited my parents, a short trip by bus and train. They—especially my father—were interested in hearing my stories and complaints about different professors and about the food at the hostel dining hall. After a couple of days of recharging at home, I would return to campus and get back to the grind.

By my second year, I began to adapt to life at the hostel. My classmates were beginning to chart out their future course of action, some wanting to obtain their Masters of Business Administration, preparing to go abroad, or seeking positions in chemical and pharmaceutical companies. In India, there was no such thing as enjoying the moment; it was always about the future. *What are we going to do next?* I was confused about what to do with my life; I was not sure whether to pursue a career in academics or become a pharmaceutical representative working for a multinational pharma company.

During the final semester, we had to prepare and defend our master's theses in an exam, called a *viva*, short for *viva voce*, meaning that the exam is oral, rather than written. In Spanish and Italian, *viva* is defined as "long live" and is used to express approval. Though the word sounds optimistic, many of classmates felt that their performance in front of the panel of professors would make or break their future careers. Some had been preparing and rehearsing for weeks; I thought they were wasting their time. Others were having nervous breakdowns. The *viva* involved no original research; we had to read different papers published in journals and give a presentation. For my topic, I chose organic semiconductors, as I was becoming interested in solid-state chemistry.

Finally, the day arrived. Each *viva* lasted about thirty to forty minutes, and each of us was assigned a time slot. We all waited outside the room while one person presented. It was like an inquisition: You enter a room and are grilled by few professors whose goal was to let you know what a fool you are. Some of my classmates came out of the room smiling, or rushed out saying, "I am going to Hollywood," like on *American Idol*; others exited with their heads down, clearly disappointed. My presentation did not have a clear beginning, middle, or end. At least, that was what one professor said; I would say that this professor did not have time to read my thesis. Another professor said that perhaps academics was not my forte and that I should work in an industry; most likely, this professor did not know anything about academics or industry. A third professor said my topic was interesting, but the field was very new and not fully established. Interpretation: "we are 'old farts'; don't expect us to learn new things." After my *viva*, I didn't come out of the room shouting "I am going to Hollywood" or feeling too down or dejected, but I was even more confused about what to do with my future. The good thing was that I had passed the *viva*.

On our last day on campus, the cooks, servers, and dishwashers prepared a celebratory last dinner at the mess hall, beginning with some drinks and munchies before the meal. I told them that my parents were expecting me for dinner, but they tried to persuade me to have a glass or two, enjoy the munchies, stay for dinner, and go home the next day. I decided that I would have a drink and then go home. I had a glass; it was a delicious drink—it tasted like *badam kheer* (almond drink). I had a second glass. While I was sipping my third glass, one of my friends advised that I should not go home that evening, explaining that the drink was called a *bhang thandai* and that it may contain some hallucinogenic ingredients. I didn't know what he was talking about, and said I was feeling fine and going home.

It was a very warm summer evening. As I sat in the back seat of a taxi, a slight breeze blew through the window. I felt drowsy and probably high (but this was a sensation I was experiencing for the first time in my life), but I was trying to fight it; I became paranoid and asked the driver to stop and let me out. It was a bit late when I finally got home, and my parents were waiting for me. I had become delirious. I told my father that I drank something at the mess hall before I left and that I was hallucinating; I remember telling him that they should stop serving this drink at school. After talking to our doctor, my father immediately decided to admit me to a private hospital. (The public hospital authorities would contact the police, our doctor warned him.) At the hospital, they gave me a stomach pump, intravenous fluid, etc. My father spent the whole night sitting next to me, making sure I was breathing. I was discharged the next day, feeling fine.

Bhang thandai is a cold drink prepared from whole milk, almonds, fennel seeds, watermelon kernels, rose petals, pepper, poppy seeds, cardamom, saffron, cannabinoids, and sugar. This drink is consumed mainly in the northern parts of India. *Bhang* has been used for centuries in India to manage pain, muscle spasms, and even seizures.

Going to a hospital probably was an overreaction, but I had not heard of THC (tetrahydrocannabinol) and wasn't familiar with its psychoactive effects. I was totally clueless about *bhang* since I grew up in the south. I learned that THC's effects peak within two to three hours of ingestion and last about six to twelve hours, depending on how many glasses of *bhang* were consumed. It wasn't until nearly a decade later when I was preparing for the American Board of Toxicology certification exam, that I learned that the difference between a drug and a poison, is the dose. Well, everything in moderation, including moderation! You live and learn!

During that summer, I moved in with my parents. I didn't do anything for a month, and they began to worry. After a few unsuccessful interviews, I was hired as a technical development chemist at a pharmaceutical company, Ciba-Geigy of India Ltd. (CIBA), in Bombay. The parent company was in Basel, Switzerland. Now, it is Novartis, one of the largest pharmaceutical companies in the world. CIBA manufactured personal products including toothpaste, talcum powder, moisturizers, anti-wrinkle cream, makeup, makeup removers, and related products. In addition, they supplied the raw materials used to make hormones, fertility drugs, and antifertility drugs as well as natural products, antibacterial drugs, and antiviral drugs.

I worked in the technical development branch, which was different from the research and development branch. Our task was to modify and scale up the synthetic procedure (from a few milligrams to kilograms of drugs) developed by scientists working in Basel. We needed to modify the solvent system to suit the conditions of storage and use in Bombay. In Basel, the procedures were developed to synthesize a one- to two-gram quantity, so we needed to revise the procedures such that several kilograms to tons could be made with a reasonable yield, purity, and cost. The conditions—temperature, reaction time, reflex conditions, purification, etc.—needed to be changed. I found this type of work boring and unstimulating as I didn't understand the point of what I was doing. Now, I realize the importance of this type of chemistry in the preparation of Good Manufacturing Practice (GMP)-grade drugs for US Food & Drug Administration (FDA) approval to initiate clinical trials in human subjects. As you scale up, the purity of the final product decreases. There is a delicate balance between an acceptable level of impurities, drug efficacy, and overall toxic side effects in humans. A GMP-grade drug must fulfill the safety conditions for human use set by the FDA in the United States and similar agencies in other countries. There are now companies in India, China, and elsewhere that have FDA-approved GMP conditions for this type of scale-up synthesis.

In our branch, we had a total of six chemists and several assistants called operators. Infights and power struggles were common among my colleagues. I spoke Tamil and English. The chemists spoke English most of the time, but when they didn't want me to know what was going on, they spoke Hindi, Marathi, or Gujarati, the commonly spoken local languages in Bombay. Another guy from South India spoke Malayalam, which is the official language of Kerala (a southern state of India). The operators spoke a variety of languages, but mostly Hindi, and they spoke no English. Although I enjoyed a lot of Hindi movies and music, I knew very little Hindi.

Getting to work at 8:00 a.m. every day (with a fifteen-minute grace period) required extreme time management, a lot of discipline, and some luck. My commute involved taking a bus and a train. The total travel time was variable, from an hour to hour and a half. There was no express highway between my parents' house and CIBA in 1972. If the buses were late or were full and didn't stop, I would miss my train connection. To avoid that, I had to get to the bus stop at 6:00 a.m. Fortunately, even if they were crowded, the trains would stop at the station for up to a minute. Most of the commuters would travel in third class instead of first because the fares were much cheaper. Though it was possible to get in and out of the first class within a minute, it was nearly impossible to get into the third-class compartments in that time. Usually, there was standing room only in even the first-class compartments. Migraine headaches from the stress of travel, noise, and pollution were almost a daily occurrence for me.

At work, we had a morning coffee break, a lunch break, and an afternoon tea break. Most companies in India followed the old British system. There were separate facilities for the operators, staff, and executives. No one brought a lunch to work; however, upon entering the lunchroom at noon, there were rows of *dabbas* (multi-compartmentalized cylindrical aluminum or stainless-steel containers, or lunch boxes) containing freshly made, home-cooked food from each employee's home. Each morning around nine o'clock, the *dabbawalas* (meal couriers) picked up more than 200,000 freshly made lunches from customers' homes and transported them by bicycle and train to the customers' respective workplaces before lunch. After lunch, the *dabbawalas* collected the empty *dabbas* and returned them to the respective homes before the customers had returned from work. This happened all over Bombay.

The *dabbawala* industry, unique to Mumbai, originated in 1890 when a massive influx of migrant workers moved to the city. The workers left early in the morning and got home late, and often didn't have lunch. There was no fast food or canteens in those days, and the workers were from different communities with palates that were satisfied only by their own, home-cooked meals. Mahadeo Havaji Bacche, a banker, wanted a home-cooked meal at work so he hired someone to deliver it to him. The idea took off, and he hired 100 meal couriers to deliver meals to nearby offices (Mumbai Dabbawala). The business, Mumbai Dabbawala, became exponentially successful.

The *dabbas* themselves are labeled with little identifying information: No address or details. The secret to getting a particular *dabba* to the correct location and back is the *dabbawala* coding system, which can be understood by the semiliterate couriers.

Harvard Business School studied the operation, logistics, and inner workings of the *dabbawala* system. All *dabbas* should be of standard size, and all *dabbawalas*, or couriers, wear the same type of clothing and a white cap. After they ring a doorbell, the *dabba* must be handed to them in less than sixty seconds. Mumbai Suburban Railway, one of the most heavily used urban commuter lines in the world, is key to *dabbawala's* success. *Dabbawalas* travel after rush hour in the morning and before rush hour in the evening. After the *dabbas* are picked up, they are brought by *dabbawala* to the nearest train station, sorted, and placed into wooden crates according to their destinations. Another *dabbawala* picks up the *dabbas* from the train station closest to the workplace and delivers them by cart or bicycle to the right offices before lunchtime. Each *dabba* is handled by six *dabbawalas* before reaching the customer (Sengar 2018). This process—picking up the *dabbas* from the workplace and returning them to the individuals' homes—is reversed in the afternoon.

Dabbawalas have been visited by the Prince of Wales, billionaire entrepreneur Richard Branson, the US Secretary of Commerce Gary Locke, and FedEx executives, among others. In 2001, the 99.99% delivery accuracy earned the *dabbawalas Forbes* magazine's Six Sigma certification (one error for every sixteen million transactions) (Moore 2011). A *New York Times* article titled "In India, Grandma Cooks, They Deliver" captivated many celebrities.

The romantic comedy *The Lunchbox* is the first Bollywood movie by an Indian director (Ritesha Batra) that won international acclaim and had excellent reviews in the Cannes and Telluride Film Festivals. This film is centered on a rare mistake by the Mumbai *dabbawalas*. The main actor in the film was Irrfan Khan, who also appears in *Slumdog Millionaire*, *Life of Pi*, and *The Amazing Spider-Man*. Co-star Nimrat Kaur made her debut in this film. Briefly, Lla, a lonely young housewife, decides to add spice to her not-so-romantic marriage by cooking a particularly delicious lunch for her husband. However, the lunchbox does not reach her husband and ends up in the hands of a widower, Saajan. Lla, upset by her husband's lack of response to the lunch, includes a note in the next day's lunchbox asking how the lunch was; Saajan returns the empty lunchbox with a message that the food was heavenly. Lla and Saajan continue exchanging messages in the lunchboxes, and their relationship grows. If you want to know what happens, you need to watch this brilliant movie (with subtitles in English).

Prior to the COVID-19 pandemic, Mumbai had 5,000–6,000 *dabbawalas* efficiently performing nearly half a million transactions within six to seven hours each day, six days a week, and fifty-two weeks a year (excluding holidays and vacations) through any kind of weather. Because of pandemic lockdowns and restrictions on train travel, as well as an increased number of people working from home, by the summer of 2021, there were only 300–500 *dabbawalas*, many of them delivering for restaurants (Sankari 2021).

During one of our lunchtime conversations, my colleagues at CIBA encouraged me to apply for a PhD program, exactly the opposite advice my professors at IIT had given me. Baxter, one of my senior colleagues, suggested that I get my PhD in the United States, and not just an average PhD but one that would allow me to become an expert in a particular area of science. He believed that becoming an expert in an area of science would go a long way in the United States but that it might not be the right thing to do in India. According to him, if you are an expert, you can be more creative. Although Baxter had not pursued education beyond his bachelor's degree, he was quite intelligent and had acquired knowledge and wisdom on various topics. We had many interesting discussions. Baxter was a Parsi, an Indian minority group originally from Persia. India—especially Bombay—has many successful businesspeople and attorneys who are Parsi. In those days, it was rare for a friendship such as ours to exist, as Parsis typically kept company mainly with one another.

To explore the research or teaching assistantships for PhDs in various graduate schools in the United States, I went to the US Embassy's information service center. Stepping inside the air-conditioned building was pleasantly refreshing, as it was usually hot and muggy outside. An alphabetical list of books on US colleges and universities was displayed in a hall. Literally, there were hundreds of books for hundreds of universities. Not knowing where to start, I began with the A's—Adelphi, Alabama, Arkansas, Auburn, and so forth. I was looking for schools that did not require high registration fees. I applied at four or five universities, including the University of Alabama, that together had registration fees that amounted to a month's salary in *rupees* (the currency of India). For some reason, I liked the University of Alabama's booklet. Probably, the photos of the cheerleaders had something to do with that. I also liked the elephant logo on the t-shirts. There was no mention of George Wallace, then governor of Alabama, standing in front of the law school building to obstruct the entry of a Black student. That would have been a turn-off. As a backup plan, I also applied for a teaching assistantship in the Chemistry Department at the University of Texas at El Paso (UTEP). One of my classmates, Ragu, had gone to UTEP a year earlier and suggested I apply there in case I didn't receive assistance from other universities.

I thought obtaining an Indian passport would be a simple procedure, but I was wrong. The Passport Office generally opened at ten in the morning and closed at 4:00 p.m. At noon, there was an hour-long lunchbreak. I would show up at the Passport Office before 10:00 a.m. to see the passport officer. The clerk at the entrance would tell me that the officer was not in, but that he would give my passport application to the officer when he returned in the afternoon. The Passport Office was near the movie theater district. To kill time, I would go see a movie at noon, watch it until intermission, and then return to the Passport Office. The clerk would tell me that the officer had returned but then had to go out on an errand. I watched many half movies this way over a few days. Finally, I gave the clerk some money and he told me he would make sure the officer acted on my application. When I returned that afternoon, I was told that my passport would be ready the next day. Sure enough, upon returning the next day to the passport office, my passport was ready! That was a long time ago; I am sure the system has become more transparent and efficient than it was decades ago.

The PhD program in the Chemistry Department at the University of Alabama accepted my application, but because I was late in applying for financial assistance, I had to wait until later in the fall semester for a decision. That was a bummer. A day later, I was offered a teaching assistantship from the Chemistry Department at UTEP. I could not get a student visa to the United States unless I showed proof of financial support, and because I didn't have a letter of financial support from Alabama, I decided to accept the offer from UTEP. Nearly half of my classmates were accepted into PhD programs in high-ranking US and Canadian universities.

In early August 1973, I departed Bombay by Air India. My parents and some friends and relatives came to the airport to see me off. I had an overnight stay in Tokyo, and one of my relatives told me that he would make sure there was someone to take care of me at the Tokyo airport. This person was an Indian administrative officer, and had connections. When I got off the plane in Tokyo, I was surprised to be greeted by the airport manager, who made sure I got to my hotel. The next day I left for San Francisco.

My cousin, who I highly respect, was doing postdoctoral work at the University of California in Berkley. He kindly met me at the San Francisco airport and let me stay with him overnight. That evening, he went to the lab to finish up some work while I watched TV. Most of what I watched focused on the Watergate scandal and possible impeachment of President Nixon. I didn't understand anything about American politics at that time. The next day, I took the flight from San Francisco to El Paso, Texas.

Chapter 3
ONE SEMESTER IN EL PASO

"El Paso city by the Rio Grande,
A voice tells me to go and see."
—*"El Paso"* by Marty Robbins

It was hot and sunny when I arrived in El Paso, Texas. No wonder El Paso is called "Sun City"; it has an average of about 300 days of sunshine each year. The city lies across the US border from Juarez, Mexico, separated by the Rio Grande, the twentieth longest river (nearly 1,900 miles) in the world, originating in Colorado in North America. Although the rest of Texas is in the central time zone, El Paso is the only major city in the state on mountain time.

Ragu, my former classmate from the Indian Institute of Technology in Bombay who had recommended I apply at the University of Texas at El Paso (UTEP), was at the airport to greet me along with his friend, Oscar, who had a car. Ragu did not have a car; he explained that he would not drive in the United States because one of his friends had been in an accident and didn't have the right kind of insurance and after paying for the damages, he had subsequently gone broke. Oscar was nice enough to take me to the apartment where Ragu was staying, which was more like a hostel. Ragu suggested that he and I, along with Rao, another student, could share a three-bedroom apartment.

Soon after, the three of us moved to El Dorado Apartments, a luxury apartment complex for its time. The only negative thing about living there was that it was about a mile from the Chemistry Department. This was fine for Rao because he had a car. Rao was working toward his master's degree in engineering and usually went to school later in the morning. Ragu was finished with his coursework in chemistry and was working on his thesis. He only went to the university when he found a ride. My first class was at 8:00 a.m. I would start walking from the apartments along Sun Bowl Drive and would try to thumb a ride to the university; some days, a Good Samaritan would stop to pick me up.

The Chemistry Department at UTEP had excellent teachers and researchers, and was very strong in the areas of quantum, inorganic, and physical chemistry. I particularly enjoyed a class taught by Keith Pannell. Keith wanted me to work on a project under him for my master's dissertation.

It wasn't until after arriving in El Paso that I learned UTEP didn't have a PhD program, and only offered a master's degree. That was a bummer, as I did not want to spend two years on another master's in chemistry followed by another four to five years to get a PhD. Whenever I saw Keith in the hallway, he would stop me and tell me that everything was laid out and all I needed to do was to focus on a few experiments, which would take six to nine months. Keith encouraged me to meet with the chair of the department, Bill Herndon, who was highly respected and had received the Dudley Memorial Professorship in the Sciences.

In my meeting with Bill, he said he'd heard good things about me, and that after earning my master's degree at UTEP, I could get into Stanford or any of the top ten US universities for my PhD. He added that it would be much easier to get a permanent academic or industry job if I had a PhD from a top university. He cautioned that going to Alabama would be a big mistake and would not help my career. I explained my reservations and said I planned to go back to India after my PhD. Bill told me that many students coming from India have said the same thing to him, but after a year or two in the United States, they get used to the American way of life and want to stay. The longer they stay here, the harder it becomes to adjust back to the Indian way of life. I told him I would think it over.

Keith was persistent. He would talk to me about the significance of his project and how it could be published in a top journal. He was organizing a symposium in organometallics at an American Chemical Society Regional Meeting at the Civic Center in El Paso, which he said would be attended by thousands of people. Keith told me he'd invited eight top-notch researchers from all over the United States to speak at his symposium, and asked me to be the slide projector operator, saying it would be a good opportunity to meet the elites in the field and showcase my knowledge. A few days before the American Chemical Society Regional Meeting, all slide projector operators from parallel sessions were given a brief training that covered turning the projector on and off, loading slides into a carousel tray, advancing and reversing the slides, and ensuring the slide decks were numbered according to the program shown in the booklet.

The organometallics symposium ran from nine to noon in a large, dimly lit convention hall, with the projector set up in the middle of the room. The first speaker stopped by the projector, handed me his slides held together by a rubber band, and told me that they were marked. A few minutes later, a second speaker came by and introduced himself, saying that he goes on after Arthur. He and Arthur began talking about a paper. The third speaker (at least I thought he was the third speaker) gave me his slides in a slide folder and asked me to load them according to the rows. Another person gave me his slides, saying that he was the first speaker after the break. Attempting to load and organize everyone's slides became overwhelming. Keith was pumped up and getting ready to start the symposium. As the room filled with people, Keith began thanking the speakers, the American Chemical Society, and all the volunteers including me (prematurely) and then introduced the first speaker from the University of California, Los Angeles. Actually, I had a bit of a problem with his slide deck; when I took the rubber band off, a few of the slides had fallen out, and I loaded them in a panic. Fortunately, Arthur's first slide, the introductory slide, was right on. Unfortunately, the next slide was the summary, but Arthur had a good sense of humor, saying that he was going to let the cat out of the bag and tell everyone the conclusions first. The next slide was also a bit out of order, and he managed it.

Then it became a guessing game, and he was no longer in control as the presentation became disjointed. He was understandably not in the best mood as he stepped down from the podium.

Keith announced that they were running a bit behind and introduced the next speaker. Arthur came to me and asked for his slides. I didn't realize that one of his slides was left behind in the tray, which then became the first slide of the second speaker. In his opening remarks, the second speaker said he hoped the worst was over. Arthur had intended to finish his talk showing a stray bull on his farm and probably wanted to tell a joke. But the second speaker was not ready for it. He had a sense of humor as well and told everyone that he hoped his research was "no bull." The rest of his slides appeared the way he had planned, and he was clearly pleased. It was a success.

Apparently back on track, Keith introduced the next speaker with a lot more confidence. This speaker had his slides marked numerically on the right corner. I loaded the slides onto the tray without rotating the slide 180 degrees. The first slide was a nice picture of a sunset reflected on the water, but it was upside down. This speaker, too, had a good sense of humor, saying that we could appreciate the photography if we all stood on our heads! When the next slide was also upside down, it became obvious to the speaker that all his slides needed to be reloaded with a 180-degree rotation. Luckily, a guy sitting nearby came to my rescue and helped reload the slides. Everything was back to normal.

The next speaker began his talk, joking that he hoped to see his own slides. Unfortunately, he had miscalculated. He had brought his slides on another carousel, so I needed to change the slide tray, which I hadn't done. As a result, the first slide I projected was not from his talk. I replaced the carousel. Then, the ultimate disaster happened. For some unknown reason, the projector lamp began overheating and one of the speaker's data slides began to melt. One of his friends sitting in the front said, "I knew he was going to show hot data but didn't expect it to be so hot that it would melt the slide!"

After the symposium, Keith told me that my reputation as a slide projectionist had spread from the Rio Grande to the Gulf Coast. He was pissed off. I got out of the meeting as quickly as I could. I certainly didn't want to showcase any more of my talents.

Had I known then what I know now, I would have a different perspective. The rule of thumb is that you should never let the slides control your presentation, as they are just a visual aid. The biggest visual aid is you, the presenter. Even when tested ahead of time, PowerPoint presentations from personal computers don't always go smoothly. And you should never assume that everything will go exactly as planned.

A few years ago, I was asked to speak at an international meeting in São Pedro, Brazil. All speakers were instructed to give their flash drives to the projectionist or email the slides ahead of time, so the files would be ready for everyone to check, and all the speakers had to do was click and present. Everything went smoothly until the keynote speech by a high-profile scientist from Johns Hopkins University in the United States. He didn't want anyone else to control the slides because his talk contained unpublished results. He'd brought a Mac laptop computer and the connecting cables with him and told the projectionists that he had everything under control. However, there was a glitch. He could see the slides on his computer but could not project them onto the screen. This was a thirty-minute talk before lunch by the poolside, and it was a nice, sunny day. After fifteen minutes, he was still unable to project onto the screen.

People started to exit. I was one of them. Only a handful of people remained in the big auditorium to listen to the special lecture.

On the other side of the coin, the famous scientist Irwin Fridovich gave presentations during which he told stories about his research. As a pioneer of redox research, Irwin and his graduate student, Joe McCord, discovered the enzyme superoxide dismutase that detoxifies the reactive oxygen species, superoxide. He was invited to the Medical College of Wisconsin for a campus-wide biomedical/biochemical symposium. Irwin began telling his superoxide dismutase story— it was relaxed, articulate, folksy, and captivating. About forty-five minutes into his talk, he apologized to the projectionist for not using his slides. He was a class act and didn't need the slides as an audiovisual aid. He was the audiovisual aid. Irwin passed away in 2019 at the age of ninety. He was a great friend and mentor, and a superb scientist.

Following the slide projection debacle at the American Chemical Society meeting, my decision to get out of Texas was made.

I must talk about the trip that Rao and I took during the Thanksgiving holiday. Ragu was very outgoing and would always share stories about the places he had seen on his various trips around the United States. Rao was more conservative, and a bit older and wiser than Ragu and me. He had left a high-paying job in India because he wanted to get his master's in engineering and then start his own company in India. Rao's wife and children were in India. He and Ragu had different views on many issues.

A few days before Thanksgiving, Rao asked me if I wanted to go with him somewhere away from El Paso. He said he would drive and that we'd share the expenses. Rao asked me to pick a place, and I chose Las Vegas. The day before we left, I got directions and told Rao we where we were going. Rao was psyched up. It was a nice drive. Rao told me about the battles between Spain and Mexico that took place in that region. We stopped by a few places like Las Cruces and Truth or Consequences. We took our time and were in no hurry.

We approached Las Vegas late in the afternoon. We saw a sign for Las Vegas once but didn't see any others. We began wondering if we'd missed an exit, so we stopped at a gas station and asked the attendant for directions to Las Vegas, explaining that we were from India and went to school in El Paso. He asked us, "What is happening in Las Vegas? Why do you want to go see Las Vegas?" I told him that we drove all the way from El Paso to see the neon lights and glitzy Las Vegas city at night. The attendant informed us that we were close to Las Vegas, New Mexico, and that nothing was happening there. We would have to cross the state of Arizona to get to Las Vegas, Nevada, which was about 700 miles away. The attendant handed us a map of the United States, lecturing that we should become familiar with the road map before venturing out. Rao didn't appreciate being lectured by a gas station attendant. It was bad on my part not to have looked at the US map closely.

When Rao started the car, something was wrong. He knew immediately that it was a transmission problem. We returned to

El Paso to Las Vegas. Map courtesy of Vecteezy.com

the gas station and the attendant told us that it was too late in the evening to fix the car but he could have it done the next morning. He suggested a cheap motel nearby where we could spend the night. I convinced Rao that it would be okay to spend a few bucks and get a decent night's sleep.

Rao was in a better frame of mind the next day. I had looked at the map and suggested places like Santa Fe and Albuquerque that we could visit on the way back to El Paso. As promised, the car was repaired, and the gas station attendant recommended we see Sandia Peak near Albuquerque. We stopped at New Mexico's capital city, Santa Fe, which was founded as a Spanish colony. Santa Fe is situated 7,000 feet above sea level, making it the highest and oldest capital city in the United States. The city is enriched with cultural and artistic influences from Hispanic, Anglo, and Native Americans. We could have spent a lot more time in Santa Fe, but we wanted to get to Sandia Peak before heading back home.

The Sandia Peak Aerial Tramway, located near Albuquerque, takes you from the city to the ridgeline of the Sandia Mountains. At times, the mountains had a pinkish color; *sandia* in Spanish refers to "watermelon." The tramway ride took about fifteen minutes, climbing over 4,000 feet to Sandia Peak. The scenery was spectacular. As we reached the top, there were restaurants and bars at the Sandia Peak ski area, and I saw snow for the first time in my life. Rao and I spent some time at the restaurant. People suggested we stay to watch the sunset, which they said would be stunning, but Rao was anxious to get back. We were the only people in the cable car going down. I wondered what would happen if there were an electrical failure, and we were stuck in the middle. Rao told me that such things don't happen in the United States. It was reassuring to hear those words from an engineer. A few months ago, I read that twenty-one people were trapped on the Sandia Peak Tramway thousands of feet in the air for twelve hours overnight until their rescue. Fortunately, our descent was uneventful.

Our trip back was smooth and without any more car problems. We returned safely to El Paso.

It's too bad that we didn't have Alexa or Siri in those days. I would have asked Siri when we left El Paso, "Siri, how far is Las Vegas?" And Siri would have asked me, "Which Las Vegas are you referring to?" I would have answered, "Siri, the Las Vegas with lots of nightclubs, casinos, and neon lights." Siri would have responded, "You want Las Vegas, Nevada. Continue northwest for 730 miles." That would have been the end of our trip because Rao would have said, "That's too far," and we would have gone somewhere closer.

We didn't tell Ragu about our attempted Las Vegas trip. He was happy to hear that we had visited Santa Fe and Sandia Peak.

Even after I informed Keith of my decision to go to Alabama, we were on good terms and became good friends. Keith is an excellent communicator. Recently, I found out that Keith has been co-hosting the *Science Studio* radio program every Sunday on El Paso's public radio station, KTEP 88.5 FM. He moderates discussions from experts on health, the environment, drug discovery, bench-to-bedside applications of drugs, therapies, medical discoveries, and a broad range of biomedical science topics. These thirty-minute, weekly segments discussing how science impacts people here and around the world have become one of the most popular science programs on KTEP radio.

The day before I planned to leave El Paso, Keith invited me, Ragu, and another friend to his house for dinner, drinks, and a poker game. We had a great time. After a nice dinner and a few beers, we began to play poker. I didn't know that we were going to play for real money. The maximum bet started off as a quarter and then rose to $5. Lady Luck was not on my side. By the end of the night, I'd lost some money.

I could not afford the plane ticket from El Paso to Tuscaloosa, Alabama, so I decided to take the Greyhound bus. It stopped in several cities including at the Union Passenger Terminal in New Orleans. By then, it was evening. As the bus drove past the Superdome, I overheard a conversation about the game between Alabama and Notre Dame that was going to take place in a few hours. Someone said they hoped that "the Tide would roll past the Fighting Irish." It was all Greek to me. After the long and grueling bus ride, I could not wait to get off the bus in Tuscaloosa.

Chapter 4

TUSCALOOSA: HOME OF THE CRIMSON TIDE

"They got a name for the winners in the world.
I want a name when I lose.
They call Alabama the Crimson Tide.
Call me Deacon Blues."
—Walter Becker and Donald Fagen of Steely Dan

The song "Deacon Blues" is from Steely Dan's 1977 album, *Aja*. In his interview for *The Wall Street Journal*, writer Marc Myers reported on how Walter Becker and Donald Fagen of Steely Dan created the story of "the expanding man" in "Deacon Blues" and the chorus line, "They call Alabama the Crimson Tide. Call me Deacon Blues." According to the interview, the song is not about a guy who achieves his dream but about the broken dream of a broken man living a broken life. Becker and Fagen wanted a grandiose name for the nerds and losers. They were sitting in a room overlooking the Pacific Ocean, watching the waves crash, when Fagen had a eureka moment: "If a college football team like the University of Alabama could have a grandiose name like the 'Crimson Tide,' the nerds and losers should be entitled to a grandiose name as well." The loser, "Deacon Blues," is not to be confused with Wake Forest University's football team, the Demon Deacons, who had a losing record at the time. Although it may be easy to associate losers with the Demon Deacons, Fagen emphasized that the deacon in "Deacon Blues" came from another source (Myers 2015). Well, that's the story of the Crimson Tide in "Deacon Blues."

Tuscaloosa is located on the banks of the Black Warrior River in the western part of Alabama and is home to the University of Alabama. I arrived at the Tuscaloosa bus station just before midnight on December 31, 1973. My brother was there to pick me up, and he was not happy.

He told me that most people don't use Greyhound service for long-distance travel and was puzzled as to why I did not fly, but then began talking about the Sugar Bowl game and why Alabama should have won. He said Alabama had the Fighting Irish backed up on the three-yard line and it was third and eight and on and on. The game would have been tied at 24–24 had Alabama's kicker—who had not missed an extra point in the last fifty or so games—gotten the extra point, but he missed it, and the Irish won 24–23. Unfortunately, I could not be empathetic as I didn't fully grasp the significance of Alabama losing a football game. Apparently, this was a dream matchup in college football's national championship game. I didn't know at the time that football is a way of life at Alabama, and practically a religion at Notre Dame; I learned this shortly thereafter.

I moved in with my brother who was living in a one-bedroom apartment in a multistory apartment complex, Rose Towers, popularly known as "Roach Towers." Most people who lived in that complex were graduate students, postdoctoral fellows, or staff workers at the university. When we got on the elevator, there was broken glass from a small TV—clearly, someone did not like the outcome of the game. I did not realize then that over the next fifty years, I would become just as passionate about, and loyal to, the Alabama football tradition.

My brother worked on superconducting polymer molecules as a postdoctoral fellow in Chuck Pittman's lab in the Chemistry Department at the University of Alabama. Although the department was within walking distance of the apartment, sometimes my brother would give me a ride there.

I was in the Chemistry Department at 8:15 a.m. the next day. Lowell Kispert, my thesis advisor, said, "Well, here he is. Supposed to show up fifteen minutes ago. We have been waiting for you." He then said that I need a nickname and suggested "Raman" because he could relate it to Raman spectroscopy. Sir Chandrasekhara Venkata Raman (from the Indian Institute of Science in Bangalore, also known as Bengaluru, India) received the Nobel Prize in 1930 for discovering a new field of spectroscopy.

Kispert told me that he worked Monday through Saturday from 7:00 a.m. to 9:00 p.m., and on Sunday, came to work in the afternoon. He asked me to try to follow his work schedule. On Saturday mornings, he held a lab meeting at 9:00 a.m. in a classroom. In the early days, it was just him and me. He would discuss publications by other groups about subjects similar to his field of study. Sometimes, he would give me papers a few days ahead, and ask me to discuss them at those meetings, presenting them from the podium next to the blackboard. I would say, "No, I can't. I'm too nervous and worried I'll make a fool of myself," and I would discuss them sitting on the chair, to which Kispert would remind me that only he was in the room and he did not care whether I impressed him. He once said, "If you don't practice speaking from the podium facing the audience, you will always be afraid to make presentations in your future career."

I was certain that giving seminars and introducing speakers would not be my future career, but he insisted I make the presentations. When presenting, I would repeat what the authors had described and would finish in ten minutes. I would not impart any of my insights or raise questions concerning the quality or the significance of the work. Like the famous slogan "All the News That's Fit to Print" that still appears in the masthead of *The New York Times*. For me, if it appeared in print, it was gospel.

Kispert instructed me to be critical, talk about the paper's strengths and weaknesses, and evaluate it as if I were a reviewer. I was not to take everything for granted; I had to raise questions. What questions are the authors answering? Are they advancing the field? Can the work be reproduced by other investigators in their labs? Are the results interpreted properly? What are my interpretations? Can the technique used in the work be applied to my research problem? Are the graphics and figures of high quality? Kispert told me to make eye contact with the audience when presenting, which I was uncomfortable doing at first. This was our routine every Saturday morning.

Kispert taught me the importance of networking. He would take me to regional meetings, making sure we were there for the social reception, and then introduce me as his graduate student to the "big shots" in the field. Slowly, I became comfortable hobnobbing and having a few beers while talking to others about their research.

Kispert instructed me to ask questions after research presentations. When I explained I was afraid to ask questions others would consider as dumb, I was told that the only dumb question was the one I did not ask. Slowly but surely, I became confident to stand up and ask questions.

He presented a key paper recently published in a high-impact journal (*Journal of Chemical Physics*, *Journal of the American Chemical Society*, *Journal of Physical Chemistry*, etc.).

He subscribed to these journals, and every other week, a new issue would be in his mailbox.

Sometimes, he would present his own paper and tell me how much time he spent in the lab and how long it took to come up with a story. I didn't think I would ever be a co-author of one of those papers. For Kispert, research was all about hard work. His mantra was, "success is 10% inspiration and 90% perspiration." Gradually, I began spending more time in the library looking at new issues of journals that were relevant to the field.

I was supported by grants Kispert received from the US Department of Energy. The funding agency was interested in finding out more about how x-radiation affects small molecules called amino acids. If this seems esoteric to most of you, that's because it is. I could not interpret the data. Free radicals (unstable and reactive species) are formed from x-radiation. Radiation kills cancer cells mainly through formation of free radicals. So, from the point of basic radiation chemistry and cancer biology, it is important to identify the nature of free radicals from irradiated biological molecules and the reactions induced by them. The gold standard technique used to identify free radicals is electron spin resonance, also known as electron paramagnetic resonance. This technique gives the fingerprints of free radicals. Understanding their fingerprints will help deduce their identities. However, not all free radicals are equally reactive. The more reactive free radicals are trapped by antioxidant molecules (e.g., vitamins E and C) to make a less reactive form of free radicals (e.g., vitamin E radical) that can be recycled back to vitamin E, for example, or decay to a relatively harmless product. My research project was centered on finding how small molecules related to chlorinated and fluorinated chemicals are damaged by radiation and determining the identity of free radicals generated in single crystals. Despite working on the project for about two years, I did not make any progress. Typically, the end of two years marks roughly the halfway point of PhD training, and I was nowhere near that. I had to choose between changing my project or my advisor. I did not want to start all over because my goal was to get my PhD within four years and go back to India.

After my first semester, my brother returned to India. I always respected my brother and was lonely and sad for a while after he left. To share the rent, I took on roommates. They were from different countries, and living with them provided interesting and unforgettable experiences for me and hopefully for them.

Tuscaloosa was pretty much a university town. Mainly, I stayed on campus and spent time with some of my friends from India; I didn't experience any racial bias. However, I had a different—albeit interesting—experience when I ventured off campus. One summer morning, I went out alone to a café in downtown Tuscaloosa. I think it was called the Drew City Coffee House. A few middle-aged White guys were sitting at a table. I took a seat away from them. I sat there for a while, looking at the menu. A White waitress and a Black waitress were standing around, but neither of them came to take my order; finally, I asked them why. Clearly, there was a misunderstanding. It turns out, they didn't know if I was Black or White. Karen thought Colleen would go to my table, and Colleen thought it was Karen's table. I told them I am from India and am a graduate student at the university. After that, both of them came to the table, asked me if I needed a refill, and told me it was free. I stayed much longer, and the two servers kept returning to the table to talk to me. As I was leaving, one of the White guys asked me, "Boy, how did you manage to get both waitresses to serve you?" I told him, "I want my coffee black with cream." I wasn't sure if they understood what I meant, but they laughed. I heard both Karen and Colleen say, "'Preciate it! Y'all come back!" I was happy to be appreciated and didn't think anything more about the encounter.

During my two years in Tuscaloosa, I made several friends, undergraduate and graduate students, who were working with an X-ray crystallographer, Jerry Atwood, who was a professor in the Chemistry Department. X-ray crystallography is an analytical technique that determines the structure of molecules and their arrangement in solids. How molecules and atoms are arranged in a solid determines their nature. For example, even though graphite and diamond are made of carbon atoms, the way the carbon atoms are arranged determines their properties. Diamond is very hard (ten on a scale of one through ten) and graphite is soft.

Diamond does not conduct electricity, but graphite does. Diamonds are a girl's best friend and graphite is not! Thus, differences in the molecular structure of a material make all the difference—whether it is a diamond or charcoal. A few years ago, I heard a rabbi, a spiritual leader in Judaism, use the same analogy at a *bar mitzvah*. I thought it was a clever idea to bring chemistry into a life lesson.

Jerry was a leading researcher in his field. We became good friends. He and everyone in his lab often worked late. I usually stopped by their lab late at night to chat; then, we'd go for a beer and play pinball and shuffleboard or go bowling. Inevitably, we would close the bar. I would be back to my lab at 8:00 a.m., and Jerry and the rest would come in at noon. Although I was not making much progress in my research, I was enjoying friendship and camaraderie with Jerry and his brilliant lab members, Ben, Rich, and Bill.

Late one afternoon in the summer of 1976, I was sitting on the steps outside of the Lloyd Hall Chemistry Department building. Usually, during summer sessions, not many American undergraduate students and only a few foreign students were on campus. A pickup truck pulled up in front of the building. Ben and Rich got out of the truck and asked me if I was interested in two for one (aka double bubble). I assumed they were going to a bar we frequented called Down the Hatch on University Boulevard, a mile or so from campus, and agreed to go, but said I had to be back in an hour to finish up an experiment in the laboratory. Ben said, "No problem." I got into the truck, and Ben asked me if I would like to go to a bar in Meridian, Mississippi, where you could get a sixteen-ounce Coors Light beer on tap. Not knowing that Meridian is roughly 100 miles from Tuscaloosa, I said, "That sounds great," while also realizing whatever research I had planned that evening was not going to happen. Rich was driving, and both Ben and I were in the back of the truck.

On I-59 South, a Mississippi state trooper stopped us. Rich asked him, "What is happening, officer?"

The officer replied, "Y'all seen a Black guy in an orange blazer along the highway, hitchhiking or somethin'?" A Black man had escaped from the prison in Meridian. "Do you have anyone else in the back?"

"Two of my friends, Ben and Raman," replied Rich.

The officer asked, "Say what? Is one of them Black or Mexican?"

To which Rich replied, "Not quite!" The officer then waved us off. I was glad he did not shine the flashlight into the back of the truck. We continued going south on I-59.

Ben asked me if I had ever been to New Orleans, and I answered, "No."

He then said, "You are going to love Bourbon Street, and all the bars and nightclubs. The party never stops." I was fine with that, as I was confident I would get back to the Chemistry Department in Tuscaloosa by noon the next day, although I knew I might have some explaining to do to my professor.

I did not have any money, not even my wallet, which was on my desk in the office. Ben said not to worry; his dad had given him a credit card as a gift for graduation, and I told him how grateful I was. We were pretty much the last people to leave Bourbon Street around 5:00 a.m., and as we were walking toward the truck, Rich said he needed to make a phone call to his grandmother in Monroe, Louisiana. He came out of the telephone booth and told us his grandmother wanted all of us to visit and have dinner with her. Rich had not seen her in a while, so we were on our way to Monroe, Louisiana! Rich explained that Monroe is located in the northern part of the state, about 280 miles from New Orleans. Before we reached her house, Ben stopped the truck at a Sears department store and asked for my underwear size. He picked up a pair of shorts and some shirts, and other things like a toothbrush. After our dinner with Rich's grandmother, Ben and Rich wanted to get back on the road. I thought that was very nice of them, so I could be back in the Chemistry Department by noon the next day. In conversation, Ben asked me if there was any place in the United States I wanted to see, as it was a great opportunity for me to see the country. I told him that I had always wanted to go to Las Vegas; he thought it was a good idea since he liked to play poker. At that moment, I realized that Ben and Rich had planned this "kidnapping" for some time. I decided to enjoy the ride. We even stopped at the Grand Canyon on the way to Vegas, spending thirty minutes looking at one of the great marvels of the world. At the gift shop, I bought a postcard, wrote a note to my professor, and threw it in the mailbox; I didn't want him to worry about me. However, that's when Ben informed me that he had talked to Bill before he left, and that Bill was going to cover for me. In those days, any kind of computing work required walking back and forth between the Chemistry Department and the Computer Center on campus. The plan was that if my professor asked about me, Bill would say, "I talked to him a few minutes ago and he is probably at the Computer Center."

We were on our way to Las Vegas, and this time it was Las Vegas, Nevada. We checked into a motel, cleaned up, and went to a casino. Ben loved to play the game seven-card stud. We stayed in Vegas a couple of days, and our schedule involved showering and gambling. Ben gave me some money. I didn't tell him about my poker fiasco in El Paso when I lost my plane fare and had to settle for a Greyhound bus. In those days, if you were playing at a card table or any machine, the drinks were free. Rich found some coupons for "two for one" breakfast at a nearby restaurant, but Ben told us how much he'd lost and that he was ready to leave Vegas.

Ben wanted to visit one of his relatives in San Francisco, but first, we decided to see the City of Angels: Los Angeles, California.

It was a difficult drive from Vegas to LA. Unfortunately, I could not help with the driving as I had not yet learned how to drive, let alone drive a stick-shift truck. Ben and Rich had been driving for many hours and wanted to get some shut-eye, so we pulled the truck over to the side of the six-lane highway in Los Angeles.

A sheriff pulled behind the truck and turned his lights on. He asked me, "What is all this with the flag?" and pointed at the back of the truck. I did not know what he was talking about. Rich explained to the officer that I was new to this country and didn't know about the Confederate flag. Clearly, the sheriff was not amused. He said quietly, "You guys should get the hell off my freeway before I take you all downtown. Don't you guys know that sleeping on the LA highway is illegal?" Rich thanked the officer, and we were then off to San Francisco, where Ben told us we could stay at his cousin's house. Ben thought it would be great to take Ventura Highway from the famous song of that name by the band America. We had the munchies and picked up a pizza. While on the scenic drive along US 101, Ben played the song Ventura Highway. Trust me, we were definitely not "chewing on a piece of grass," but the day definitely felt longer. We then followed the Pacific Coast Highway all the way to San Francisco. It was a spectacularly scenic road trip.

We stayed that night with Ben's cousin, a nice woman who welcomed us into her home. The next morning, after a nice breakfast, we left San Francisco. Ben thought he could recoup some of his Vegas losses and suggested we spend a few hours at a casino in Reno, Nevada, so that's what we did. But Lady Luck was not on our side, and we decided to head on out. Ben suggested that it would be nice to see Salt Lake City in Utah; we stopped and spent a few more minutes there than we had at the Grand Canyon.

After the long drive, we needed to rest and checked into a motel in Cheyenne, Wyoming. I turned on the TV and was pleasantly surprised to see *The Cheyenne Social Club*. I thought it was coincidental, but Ben told me that it was an advertisement for Cheyenne. Later I found out that this movie, initially released in 1970, is an American comedy Western about an aging cowboy who finds out that the business he inherited from his brother is actually a brothel. The movie has an impressive cast, including James Stewart, Henry Fonda, Shirley Jones, and a host of others.

As we were leaving Cheyenne, Ben decided he wanted to see his aunt in Madison, Wisconsin. She was a politician, probably a representative in the state legislature. After another long drive, we arrived in Madison and had lunch with Ben's aunt at a restaurant, frequented by congressional representatives, near the Wisconsin State Capitol. The restaurant dress code required wearing a nice red jacket. I remember even the extra-small sized jacket was too large for my 120-pound physique, making it difficult to avoid dipping my sleeves into the soup. Ben's aunt introduced us to her fellow legislature friends, who mostly discussed the upcoming election. After lunch, we drove through Milwaukee, and Ben explained to me that it was called the beer capital of the world—little did I know that I would later spend more than half of my life in Milwaukee.

Finally, after two weeks and 6,000 or so miles of cross-country travel, I was back in the Chemistry Department. When I saw my professor, he greeted me with, "So you're back." He was happy to have received my postcard and began telling me all about Grand Canyon National Park, the red rocks, and their geological history. He also talked of his hike down the canyon to the Colorado River and the Phantom Ranch. I didn't mention that I spent only thirty minutes at the Grand Canyon. I was relieved that he was not mad at me.

"Kidnapping" trip route. Map image courtesy of vecteezy.com.

During the trip, something positive happened related to my research project. Ben asked me about my research; I explained it was not going well and that my clock was ticking, as I had been there for nearly two years and things were not clicking on the research front. Ben suggested I change the project or join Jerry's research group and work on solving crystal structures by X-ray crystallography. For a few weeks, I considered what he'd said. Maybe he was right. To paraphrase Abraham Maslow's quote, if the only tool you have is a hammer, you tend to see every problem as a nail; I realized I should try a different tool rather than changing the nail.

In one of our late-night bar-hopping sessions, I asked Jerry if he would help me with the crystal structure determination of my compound. Jerry said it was no problem. The next day, I brought a small crystal of my compound to his lab, and the automated machine started collecting the data that would show the electron density map from which the structure could be determined. Usually, it took several hours to collect the data, and determining the structure of a small molecule like mine would take at most a week.

From the electron density map, one obtains the likely coordinates of the various atoms in the molecule and then uses a computer program to optimize the structure with a parameter called R. If the value of R is between 0 and 5 or so, you know you're on the right track. The R value was around 70 on my first try. My next step was to try other combinations of coordinates; this went on for a few months, and Kispert was getting anxious. I told him if I could determine the structure, I would be able to complete the project. A few days before Christmas 1976, during our late-night bar hopping, I told Jerry things looked bleak and there was no way I could finish my PhD project unless I figured out the crystal structure. He said, "Damn, Raman, I have never seen anyone working so tirelessly on a problem and not give up—let me take another look at the electron density map." He then told me, "I think we have a disordered crystal structure. We need to treat this as if we have two molecules superimposed." He drew some circles on the electron density map and then went home. I went to the lab and tried various combinations of coordinates of atoms for a disordered-type molecule, and then made the chilly hike to the Computer Center on one of the coldest nights of the year. I left the card deck containing the coordinates with the operator and went home. The next day, I came into work a bit later than usual and headed to the Computer Center to look at the results. The R factor was down to 4 or so. Jerry was right. In the next month, I solved a few more structures using the same approach and related the crystal structure to other spectroscopic results! I had used a different hammer (X-ray crystallography) to interpret the electron paramagnetic resonance results.

It was probably one of the most trivial scientific problems in the world, but for me, it was momentous. It meant I could finally make a reasonably sound scientific story explaining the problem and interpreting the results. It was a turning point in my research life with regard to my self-confidence and belief in my creative thinking. I was the first author of several publications in highly respected journals. Kispert told me that I was ready to get my PhD. The path to earning a PhD involves developing scientific training, logical progression, repeating and reproducing results, and interpreting the results uniquely and differently, supported by experimental evidence. During this process, which can take anywhere from three to six years, the analytical part of your brain is activated, giving way to creative thinking. A different part of the brain is activated in the field of arts. Activating both parts of the brain used for science and art is like reaching Nirvana in life.

For me, life in Alabama became all about science and football. My friends would take me to football games with them. At that time, some home games were played at the Legion Field stadium in Birmingham. One memorable game had Alabama playing Missouri, or Mizzou. I was still figuring this game out. Bear Bryant was Alabama's coach and Richard Todd was the quarterback. Calvin Culliver was the running back, and a good one. People would cheer, "Run, Calvin, run!" One time I heard the old guy sitting behind me shout, "Oh shit, oh shit!" I had not seen the play, so I turned around to ask him what happened. He said, "That boy dropped the ball!" I asked him, "You mean Calvin?" He looked at me as if I was from a different planet. I told him that it was just a game and these things happen. Alabama went on to lose that game.

Alabama football started to grow on me, and soon I was a fan(atic) of the Crimson Tide. Alabama had not won a national championship in several years, and then came the 1978–1979 season. I remember the excitement of witnessing the famous "goal line stand" at the Sugar Bowl game played at the Louisiana Superdome in New Orleans on January 1, 1979. The second-ranked Crimson Tide coached by Bryant played the top-ranked Nittany Lions of Penn State coached by Joe Paterno.

About eight of us, including Bill, Rich, Jerry, and others, stayed in one room in a hotel on Monroe Street in New Orleans. The evening before the game, we went to the famous Pat O'Brien's bar, an outdoor hangout with a flaming fountain on Bourbon Street. This place is known for its Hurricane cocktail drinks made with rum and Hurricane mix and served in a glass shaped like a hurricane lamp. There were masses of partying Alabama and Penn State fans. As the night wore on, discussion and arguments regarding the outcome of the Sugar Bowl became heated. I happened to be in one of them. A Nittany Lions fan told me that they didn't have to play us, and that 'Bama was lucky to be playing against them. Apparently, Paterno wanted to play Oklahoma at the Orange Bowl during prime time, but after a few phone calls Bryant convinced him to play against 'Bama. This was in the era before computer power rankings and playoffs.

45th Annual Sugar Bowl Classic ticket, 1979. Photo credit: Bill Hunter.

I proposed a wager that if Penn State won, I would buy Hurricane drinks for them all night long after the game. If Penn State lost, they would do the same for me and my friends. A lot of 'Bama fans were rooting for me. They were wondering how in the heck a guy from India became so passionate about Alabama football. I imagine the Penn State fans were thinking differently—what a dumbass from India! Even in those days, the Hurricane drinks were expensive. I had no idea how I was going to pay for all the drinks if Alabama lost.

The game was a defensive chess match between veteran coaches, with lots of turnovers and defensive plays. Alabama was up 14–7 late in the fourth quarter. Finally, with about six minutes left in the game, Penn State put together a fierce drive and had the ball, first and goal. Then it was fourth down on the one-foot line. Paterno knew that they may not get the ball back and decided to go for it. Apparently, before the snap, Penn State quarterback Chuck Fusina had cockily asked Marty Lyons—one of the linebackers for Alabama—what play to run, and Lyons told him to throw the ball. Fusina should have listened to Lyons, but the call was to run up the middle and pick up a foot. Alabama linebacker Barry Krauss had different ideas. What happened next was the legendary "goal line stand" when Penn State was stopped for no gain. Krauss was named the game's most valuable player, Alabama prevailed 14–7, and clinched the national championship. Predictably, I didn't see any Penn State fans at Pat O'Brien's after the game.

Even after moving out of Tuscaloosa, I followed Alabama football religiously. After Bryant retired, Alabama football was not the same, and the team was not as dominant for many years until they won another national championship in 1992.

By 2007, the college football world had changed. Alabama recruited Nick Saban as the head coach. Since then, Alabama has won six national championships. I watched most of the games under Coach Saban, and I listened to what he had to say before and after the games. I became interested in how he trains and strengthens mindset through "The Process," which moves the focus away from the result to variables that are within one's control

(Lessons In Leadership Institute 2018). The principles he laid out for achieving success in football can be applied to achieving success in other areas of life—including conducting research, writing grant proposals and publications, giving presentations, teaching, and training medical and graduate students and postdoctoral fellows. Unwittingly, I might have actually applied some of his principles in my work.

Saban has coached four Heisman Trophy winners at Alabama, the latest being the first Alabama quarterback to win the Heisman Trophy. In the 2022 division championship, Alabama lost to Georgia, who hadn't won a national championship in four decades. Saban was gracious in defeat and told Georgia coach Kirby Smart, "You guys kicked our ass in the fourth quarter." Smart was the defensive coordinator at Alabama for many years before becoming the head coach of the Georgia Bulldogs.

After I successfully defended my PhD thesis in the summer of 1978, I joined the lab of Ron Mason at the National Institute of Environmental Health Sciences in Research Triangle Park, North Carolina, as a visiting postdoctoral fellow.

Chapter 5
THE THRILL IN CHAPEL HILL

Everything in life happens for a reason.
—Aristotelian philosophy

"For better, for worse, for richer, for poorer, in sickness, and in health, to love and to cherish."
–Traditional Marriage Vows

In May 1978, I arrived in North Carolina in my 1969 Ford Galaxy. I had accepted a visiting postdoctoral fellow position in the Laboratory of Environmental Biophysics at the National Institutes of Environmental Health Sciences (NIEHS), located in the Research Triangle Park (RTP), commonly known as "the Triangle." The RTP is surrounded by the cities of Durham and Raleigh, and the town of Chapel Hill, which are home to three major universities: Duke University, North Carolina State University, and The University of North Carolina at Chapel Hill (UNC).

The RTP, established in 1959, is a hub for numerous science, technology, biopharmaceutical, big pharmaceutical, and investment companies as well as government agencies. *Triangle Business Journal* reports that more than 50,000 people work in the RTP. What was a little triangle when I was there in the 1970s has since become a huge triangle.

When I first arrived in North Carolina, I stayed with Ron and Mary Mason in the town of Cary, a suburb of Raleigh, while I looked for an apartment. One apartment complex, called the Stones Throw Apartments, was located at the RTP and was within walking distance of the NIEHS. Many people who worked at the NIEHS lived in those apartments. I wanted to explore other options.

As I was driving around, trying to find a place to live, I thought of Peter Craven, who was doing his postdoctoral fellowship in the Chemistry Department at UNC and working with William Hatfield. I had met him several times at conferences I had attended with Lowell Kispert. I got in touch with Peter, and he said he would meet me for a beer at a bar called He's Not Here on Franklin Street in Chapel Hill. Peter and his roommate, Pete, who was working in the RTP, convinced me that I shouldn't live near the RTP; they suggested I find a place in Chapel Hill or Carrboro, which is located about a mile from He's Not Here. In the meantime, they offered that I could stay with them as they had an extra bed. Pete explained that nothing is happening socially at the RTP and that I would have to come to Chapel Hill for fun; he also warned that it is a bit of a drive from Chapel Hill to the RTP, and way too far to drive on the curvy two-lane NC-54 late at night. He also pointed out that driving to work with a hangover is less dangerous and not illegal; I thought his logic was impeccable. I stayed with Peter and Pete for a week, during which time I found a one-bedroom apartment at Greenbelt Apartments in Carrboro. The managers of the Greenbelt Apartments, a couple named Christine and Chad, were exceedingly friendly. I signed a one-year lease.

Next door to the apartment complex was a restaurant called the Red Baron that specialized in seafood and steak. It looked like a nice place, but when I stopped in, nobody was there except a bartender named Mike. I learned that Mike was the owner; he moved from Philadelphia and had purchased the restaurant a few days prior. He was a beer and food connoisseur and wanted to make the Red Baron a special seafood and steak place, unlike Red Lobster. Mike informed me that I was his first customer, so my first beer was on the house. The silence at the bar was deafening, and I found myself speaking louder and louder. Mike liked that, as it seemed as though the place was hopping. I told Mike he needed to get a good sound system and play some jazz. It was his top priority, he said. Mike and I became good friends. Whenever I came back to the restaurant, my first beer was on the house. That made me feel special.

I started work at the NIEHS. It is aptly named, as it's the part of the National Institutes of Health focused on the health effects of environmental chemicals in humans. Much of the research dealt with estrogenic compounds, such as diethylstilbestrol used in cows, the effect of ultraviolet radiation on skin cancer, the metabolism of environmental agents such as TCDD (also known as dioxin), aromatic hydrocarbons, and heavy metals in different organs including the lung, liver, and kidney, and the mechanism of action of nonsteroidal anti-inflammatory drugs like aspirin and Celebrex. I worked with Ron in the Laboratory of Environmental Biophysics headed by Colin Chignell; I was Ron's first postdoctoral fellow. The NIEHS was an exciting place to do research. Because I was also interested in the biological effects of radiation, I collaborated with Colin's group and helped solve some problems related to the mechanism of photodegradation of active ingredients in sunscreen lotions. Colin was a true British gentleman—he never raised his voice and was always savvy and diplomatic. I was deeply saddened when, in 2008, Collin tragically drowned due to rip tides while swimming near North Myrtle Beach, South Carolina. Ironically, Colin was the one who saved my life when Ron, Ann Motten, Colin, and I went sailing on a large, beautiful lake in New England, near a conference we were attending. Our small catamaran boat tipped over, which apparently is common for these boats. I could not swim, so I held onto the boat for dear life. Colin, an experienced swimmer and sailor, immediately swung into action and made sure I got back on the boat safely. One thing is for certain: Even the best swimmer is no match for a rip current; they are dangerous and can pull you down.

A couple days later, when I went to the Red Baron, a few people were there; some of them were firefighters. Mike was listening to a local radio station. I gave Mike a cassette tape of Bob James' *Touchdown* album that I'd gotten from a guy, Gordon, who lived in my apartment complex and was a disc jockey at the UNC radio station. He played it and the firefighters approved. The hit song "Touchdown" was popularized by the TV series, *Taxi*. From Gordon and another friend, I collected the cassettes of Grover Washington Jr., Earl Klugh, Chick Corea, the Rippingtons, Dave Sanborn, the Yellowjackets, Pat Matheny, and more. In the weeks that followed, the Red Baron became a popular seafood and steak restaurant that played jazz music. On Fridays, even I could not find a seat at the bar.

I decided I wanted to get into shape. The area I lived in was perfect for jogging, so I started going for jogs. One time, I went a bit too far. As I slowly walked back home, a car pulled up and the driver asked me if everything was alright. I explained I had just taken up jogging and did not know how to pace myself. He introduced himself as Earl and offered me a lift. I told Earl I was new to the area and that I was trying to get the lay of the land. We started talking about college basketball—I was a fan of the Crimson Tide and Earl liked the Tar Heels. Earl invited me to have a beer with him. We went to a place called Spanky's, one of the most popular restaurants and bars on Franklin Street. Earl knew everyone there, and I was in my running clothes. The owner, Mickey, came by and talked to us. Suddenly, I knew a lot more people in Chapel Hill. What started off as a thirty-minute jog turned into a six-hour outing.

Earl worked out at Eastgate Spa in Chapel Hill and invited me along as his guest. I met him around six o'clock the following night. Over the next hour, Earl took me through the different machines that worked different muscle groups. After, we went out for dinner capped off with a beer or two before calling it quits. The next day, the same thing. We did this five days a week; on Saturdays and Sundays, we would take a break from the workouts but still go jogging. After a few weeks, several people joined us during our workouts. It was intense. Our group had a lot of energy, so we were a magnet for people who wanted to work out but needed motivation.

With more people, the workouts lasted longer. The owner of the gym asked me to moonlight. I did not know what he meant, but I told him it sounded like too much work. After working out, our usual routine was to eat out and stop off for a few drinks before going home. On Sundays, we started a trend called Bloody Mary breakfasts at Spanky's. Friends from the workout club joined us. Our "breakfast" typically lasted for several hours. In 2021, nearly forty years after it opened, the iconic Spanky's Restaurant and Bar permanently closed. I was sad to learn that Mickey passed away in 2020. As mentioned in a tribute, Harrison Jennings "Mickey" Ewell "changed the look of Franklin Street" (McConnell 2020).

Each Saturday during football season, my friend Bob hosted a Bloody Mary party at his place before the game. A lot of friends from the spa would show up. Earl always made sure I had a ticket to the game, but Bob and I were more interested in the party than the game and, much to Earl's chagrin, we wouldn't arrive at the game until after the first quarter. Bob became my good friend and, after I met my wife, Lilian, we spent a lot of time with Bob.

Bob was into antiques and had a priceless Persian rug in his bedroom upstairs. The rug got bleached after Bob hired a company to clean the outdoor patio near the pool. Apparently, the workers mixed muriatic acid with bleach in a bucket in Bob's kitchen and used it for cleaning.

Bob sued the cleaning company and hired a lawyer from Chapel Hill. There was a jury trial in the nearby town of Hillsborough, and Bob asked me to be his expert witness. My compensation was a Waffle House breakfast. Mixing muriatic acid (also known as hydrochloric acid) and bleach (sodium hypochlorite) would release nascent chlorine and other oxides of chlorine that could have diffused from the kitchen area to the bedroom upstairs and reacted with the fibers of the Persian rug, causing it to bleach. Thus, I prepared my testimony for the hearing.

When I took the stand during the trial, the attorney representing the cleaning company asked me how farfetched was the claim that muriatic acid and bleach kept in the kitchen would have destroyed a rug upstairs. I told the court that it is not farfetched at all, considering that hydrofluorocarbons from hair sprays and other aerosols could go to stratosphere and react with the ozone to deplete the ozone layer, thereby enhancing ultraviolet light-induced skin cancer in humans. Despite the attorney's objection, the judge allowed me to go on as he found the story to be educational. However, the cleaning company's lawyer also had an expert witness—a professor from Duke University who had more credentials than me and was being paid for his testimony. The professor testified that he had done this experiment many times, mixing muriatic acid and bleach in freshmen chemistry labs, without any problems. One can smell a bit of a pungent odor, he said, and that is all. He did not mention the concentration of the individual substrate or anything else of that nature. In the end, the jury sided with the cleaning company. If we had physical proof, showing chlorinated products from the bleached rug, our argument would have been convincing, but we had none. Unfortunately, there was a "hole" in my theory.[2]

After Edward Perez-Reyes graduated from UNC, he joined Ron's lab as technician. He went on to become a professor of pharmacology at the University of Virginia. Ed was a quick learner and got Ron's lab going at full speed. Ron was trying to understand the hepatotoxicity of chlorinated chemicals, such as chloroform and carbon tetrachloride, and was using rat liver enzymes as a model for their metabolism in human livers. Ron taught Ed how to isolate rat liver and process it for use in subsequent investigations. Ron gave me a theoretical project that didn't go anywhere. I was getting frustrated, so I decided to work on a different project. While Ron was out of town attending a scientific meeting, I did a literature search on the metabolism of chemotherapeutic drugs like Adriamycin (also known as doxorubicin). This drug was successfully used to treat several cancers. However, its clinical use was limited due to its cardiotoxic side effects, attributed to toxic free radicals generated from its metabolism in the heart tissues. Experimental evidence clearly identifying the mechanism of this process was lacking in the literature. To investigate the metabolism of Adriamycin, I borrowed the liver tissue preparation from Ed. I worked on my project for a week and obtained interesting results, which I showed to Ron when he returned. He was impressed and asked if I had isolated and prepared the liver tissue by myself. I let Ron know that Ed had provided the liver tissues and that we would work on this project together. Ron was insistent I do the surgery and prepare the liver tissues for my project. I explained that I was a Hindu, and Hindus don't kill any living species. I had never personally killed a rat or a mouse, even though rats were a major problem in our house

2) This is a tongue-in-cheek reference to the depletion of the ozone layer in the stratosphere by hydrofluorocarbons.

in Chennai. I shared with Ron the story of how we got rid of rats when I was growing up.

Every night, my grandmother would set several rat traps around the house. If a rat was trapped, one of us would take the rat in the trap to an open field away from other houses and let it out. When it was my turn to do this, young boys in the neighborhood would recognize that I needed help and follow me. I would walk along the road a bit like the Pied Piper of Hamelin. In that tale, the mayor of the town of Hamelin hired a piper—dressed in multicolored (pied) clothing—to lure rats away with his magical pipe, thus saving the town from a deadly plague. When the Pied Piper was not appropriately compensated for his efforts, he took revenge and lured the town's children away. As the neighborhood boys followed me, they would gather rocks and prepare for me to let the rat out. These rats were not like the small, lean Charles River rats used in labs; they lived in the sewer and were typically much bigger. However, the artilleries (rocks) the boys fired got the job done.

Ron found my story amusing but insisted I should learn to do the surgery and isolate liver tissues by myself. Thus began my efforts to become a rat surgeon. Rats were either decapitated using a guillotine or anesthetized before isolating the liver. I decided to use the procedure involving anesthetics. Usually, a standard dose of anesthetics—isoflurane or halothane—was administered to rats, and the livers were isolated quickly and kept on ice for the subsequent work up. The surgeries were done before 9:00 a.m. so we could complete the whole preparation (centrifuging, protein analyses, etc.) before noon. One time, Ed was not around, and I started the procedure by myself. After administering halothane, the rat dozed off and I began the surgery. Although I had watched someone else do the procedure many times, it took much longer when I did it. After I isolated the liver, I had to go get the ice to store the tissue. I should have gotten that ready ahead of time, as it took a while to get everything organized. When I came back to euthanize the rat, I could not find it. Apparently, the anesthetics wore off and it gingerly crawled away, dragging its feet and spilling blood all over. In an adjacent laboratory, a colleague was investigating the effect of microwaves on human health. He was sitting on a chair, contemplating what to do that day, when he saw my rat near his desk; he completely lost it. When Ron found out what had happened, my days as a rat surgeon were over. He also made sure that I become conversant with ethics in animal care/surgery.

My social life after work was accelerating. One evening, I went to the office of my apartment complex to drop off my rent check. There was the ever smiling and always welcoming Christine. She said she was happy to see me, and she insisted I join her and Chad at an exciting event taking place that weekend in Raleigh.

Christine and Chad drove me to the Raleigh Civic Center for what turned out to be an Amway convention. They introduced me to a few people, one of whom showed me a $10,000 check he had received a few days earlier. I thought that was strange. The auditorium was filled with upbeat, excited people. There were a lot of motivational speakers focused on the daily grind— waking up early, going to work, making little money, and missing out on their dream vacations—and how they got out of it. One of them bragged that he shot his alarm clock after becoming a "diamond direct." Everyone understood what he meant by that; I didn't, but soon learned that a direct distributor, or "diamond direct," is the level at which you start making money. He told his audience that it costs just $100 to become financially independent. Some speakers showed pictures of people taking cruises after having reached a recruitment or sales goal. Tapes and books instructing how to achieve the Amway goals were sold to convention attendees. I learned that Amway products included cleaners, soaps, and detergents for dishwashers, upholstery, and leather car seats, among other things. The guy who showed me the $10,000 check asked me what I was doing for a living and wanted to know how much I hated my job. I couldn't relate as I was having fun working in the lab, making discoveries, working out, and socializing with friends. The attendees were instructed not to give up their day jobs until they become diamond directs, and that the best way to start selling was to contact family members, friends, and acquaintances from church; the goal was to reach a wider audience. Although I had no interest in selling Amway products, I felt that refusing meant I had wasted Christine and Chad's time, so I agreed to give it a try.

After the convention, Christine and Chad would ask me if I had recruited anyone or sold any Amway products. I did not want to disappoint them, so I spent hundreds of dollars buying my own Amway products (soap, dishwashing liquid, leather cleaner, shampoo . . . everything but the kitchen sink). Christine called me one day and suggested I stop buying products to meet my quota and instead work on other people. When I explained that I didn't know how to approach people and sell stuff, she offered to help.

The Amway direct distributor who recruited Christine and Chad contacted me and asked that I invite a few people to my apartment. He said he wanted to share some "really exciting information" and asked me not to discuss any more details. I had made several new friends over the past few months, so I invited them to a party at my apartment. I had recently bought a sound system, and Gordon turned me onto some new albums. On the night of the party, I made sure the refrigerator was full and had the necessary snacks and good music. Even though the direct distributor guy told me that he would come at 8:00 p.m., I wanted to get a head start, so friends began rolling in early. Gordon took care of the music, and my guests were rocking. Some people started doing shots right away. I could smell a nice aroma from the kitchen; I knew what it was. When the party was in full swing, I forgot that the direct distributor was going to show up.

Suddenly, there was a knock on the door. Some people became paranoid and asked me to turn down the music, thinking the police had shown up. I opened the door and there stood the direct distributor carrying a whiteboard and a whole bunch of markers. The music came back on. I introduced the guy to everyone and told them he was going to share something very exciting.

I heard someone from the kitchen say in a high-pitched voice after taking a toke, "Is that the Amway dude, man?"

"Give that guy a cold one and ask that dude to chill out!"

I told everyone to be nice and listen to our guest speaker. He placed his whiteboard in the middle of the crowded room and asked everyone, "When was the last time you were all excited?" I wish he hadn't asked that question. He didn't appreciate the lewd answers he received. He talked about Dun & Bradstreet and credit ratings and drew circles on the whiteboard showing the strategy to becoming a direct distributor. My friend from the kitchen peeked out and said, "Man, that looks like a pyramid scheme." The presentation was too much reality for a Friday night party. After sharing with everyone the secret to getting rich, the direct distributor walked out. I tried to get him to hang out and have a beer, but he was not interested. As I apologized for my friends' rude behavior, he told me I would need to change my social life if I wanted to make it big and climb the Amway ladder. That was the end of my Amway business connection.

I moved to a different apartment complex, Pine Gate Apartments, in May of 1979. This apartment complex was more luxurious than my last place and had a clubhouse and a swimming pool. Directly across from the apartment complex was a Subaru car dealership, and a friend of Earl's was a salesman there; I purchased my first new car from him.

That weekend, I decided to check out the pool. As I walked over, I heard music and saw groups of people enjoying the start of the summer of 1979. I took a spot in a corner and spent a few hours there before returning to my apartment. The next day, I walked over to the pool carrying a six-pack of Stroh's Light cans over my shoulder. That got the attention of a few people, and soon, we were friends. As we got louder, more people gravitated toward our group—no one wanted to miss out on the fun. Our poolside activities were a weekly occurrence throughout the summer and would start Friday evening and end Sunday evening. We could not wait for the weekend to arrive.

I was getting used to my lifestyle in the United States. I liked my work even though my job was not permanent, and I enjoyed my life outside of work. Still, I wanted to look for job opportunities in India. I attended a meeting in the spring of 1980 where I met a top research investigator from the Tata Institute of Fundamental Research, a premier research institute in Bombay that had worldwide recognition. I inquired about the possibility of obtaining a position at the institute. He let me know that India was saturated with people like me and that finding a job there with my level of experience would not be easy. That was not what I had expected him to say. Universities in the United States had opportunities that involved a lot of teaching and less research, but I did not have teaching experience yet. One such opportunity was in the Department of Chemistry at Clemson University, South Carolina. The chair, Rudy Abramovitch, was my organic chemistry instructor when I was a graduate student in Alabama. Rudy was a great teacher, and I still use most of the principles I learned from him in my research. He was disappointed when I told him Clemson was not the right place for me. So, I continued my research at the NIEHS. Roger Sealy, whom I'd previously met at a magnetic resonance conference, was a faculty member at the Medical College of Wisconsin in Milwaukee, Wisconsin, and had come to the NIEHS to give a seminar. I spoke with him about my situation, and he said he would be happy to offer me a postdoctoral fellowship at the Medical College of Wisconsin. This offer sounded good to me, and I said I would think it over.

In the lab, Ron and I would often argue about research and testing hypotheses. He would tell me I was good at poking holes in a hypothesis before it was tested, but I got things accomplished, and Ron and I began publishing papers. Despite our arguments, Ron and I had mutual respect for each other and have remained friends.

Finally, the summer of 1980 arrived. That meant weekends at the Pine Gate "beach," which is what we called our pool. On May 1, the pool opened, and music started blaring from the clubhouse. Like the summer before, I walked to the pool with a six-pack of Stroh's Light slung over my shoulder. The same group of people was there, and the party began. The following weekend, it was the same routine. This time, as I walked to the pool with my six-pack of Stroh's Light, I passed a few girls suntanning. One of them said I should get a cooler to keep the beer cold. I replied, "Why don't you help me finish the beer before it gets warm?" I gave them each a beer and we talked for a while; then, I left to join my friends. The next day, I returned to the pool with two six-packs of Stroh's Light. I walked past the same girls—Lilian, Deborah, Debbie, and Faye—and shared the beers with them. They lived at Pine Gate, too, in a three-bedroom apartment; Lilian, Deborah, and Faye were juniors at Greensboro College in North Carolina, which is about forty-five miles south of Chapel Hill, and were there for summer jobs. I introduced them to my Pine Gate beach friends, and they hung out with us the rest of the day.

When I asked them to join us for dinner, Lilian, Deborah, and Debbie agreed. I started a conversation with Lilian and found out that her parents came to the United States from Cuba when she was two years old, and she grew up in North Carolina. I told her about myself, and she was interested in what I had to say. Even though the place was crowded and noisy, we had no problem carrying on our conversation—we were in our own world.

Lilian had a summer job at the Wendy's restaurant across the street, and could only come to the pool after her shift was over. I told her that was a bummer, and she suggested I come to Wendy's for lunch. I felt a glimmer of hope. Having lunch at Wendy's became my routine. Lilian's coworkers took notice when I showed up; if she was not in the front taking orders, they would tell her when I arrived. She would come to my table and ask me, "How are the first few bites tasting?" When have you ever seen that happen at a fast-food restaurant? I loved going to Wendy's. Lilian and I both knew we enjoyed each other's company. At that point, the summer of 1980 was a phenomenal success.

One Sunday evening, I saw Lilian at Pine Gate beach, and she looked kind of sad. She was not her usual cheerful self, so I knew something was bothering her. All her friends were vacationing in Nags Head, a town on North Carolina's Outer Banks known for its beautiful beaches, and she had a few days off but no way to get there. Knowing I could find a ride to work, as many people who lived at Pine Gate worked at the RTP, I let her borrow my car. Lilian was ecstatic and assured me she would take care of my car as if her life depended upon it. I told her I didn't worry too much about material things and that I fully trusted her.

When I got to work the next day, I told my NIEHS colleague Birandra that I'd let Lilian take my car to the Outer Banks. He said, "You are either the dumbest guy in the world or the smartest guy in the world." And he didn't want to guess which. I knew what he was thinking, though, as the first thing he asked me every morning was, "Did you get your car back?" When I let Birandra know Lilian had returned with my car, and that she was pleased to have enjoyed camping with her friends, he said, "Raman, I have never seen you this happy."

Birandra invited me to go with him to a scientific meeting in New Orleans and offered to drive. Birandra was fine with my request to bring Lilian with us; however, I didn't initially tell him I had also invited Bill Honig, whom I knew from Alabama. I told Birandra that Lilian and I would ride in the back and Bill would be in the front seat to help navigate. Birandra was surprised to find out about the fourth person. It was a twelve-hour drive from Chapel Hill to New Orleans; to break up the monotony, we stopped in Tuscaloosa to see friends. Visiting New Orleans with Lilian was an entirely different experience. I shared my kidnapping story with her; little did she know, she would hear it hundreds of times in her life.

Following the conference, our drive back to Chapel Hill was interesting. Birandra and Bill argued about a lot of things, as they both seemed to have strong views on everything. Lilian and I sat in the backseat listening to them and then started exchanging notes. We didn't want Birandra and Bill to know what was going on, but they could tell something was up because of our giggles in between messages. Our notes went something like this:

Lilian: "I have really strong feelings for you. What about you?"

Me: "Me too."

Lilian: "You are funny. You make people laugh, and you are so confident around people."

Me: "You mean I talk funny. I only talk about things I know. I don't know a whole lot, so I make up stuff."

Lilian: "What? That does not make much sense, but I like it. What do you think of me?"

Me: "You are a natural. What you see is what you get! I like what I see! I like consistency, and you are consistent. That way, I can be who I am. No pretense."

Lilian: "Not everything in life has to make sense. Seriously, do you really like hanging out with me?"

Me: "I love it, and I live for it."

Lilian: "I feel the same. I go through the whole week thinking about the previous weekend and looking forward to the upcoming weekend."

Me: "So, what else should we talk about?"

Lilian: "I don't know much about you!"

Me: "One way to find out is to spend more time together."

Lilian: "You mean, days, weeks, months, or years."

Me: "The rest of our lives!"

Lilian: "You said you were thinking of going to work in Milwaukee!"

Me: "I'll spend a couple of years at the Medical College of Wisconsin. You can come with me."

Lilian: "My parents won't let me go with you, unless . . ."

Me: "Unless what? You mean, get engaged?"

Lilian: "Well, something like that."

Me: "Okay, how about us getting engaged?"

Lilian: "Do you really mean it? That is exciting!"

Well, our backseat sweet nothings led to our marriage. We can't blame it on alcohol, as none was used at the time of the proposal. This is not a prescription for everyone, but it worked for us. Maybe it is all about timing. Timing with no judgment!

Lilian announced our engagement to her parents and then took me to meet them. At that time, Lilian's parents, Carlos Alberto and Elisa Rodriguez, lived in Monroe, North Carolina. Lilian's father was a minister at several United Methodist churches. I relayed our plans to him. He told me that he had treated Lilian like a sensitive flower that requires a lot of attention and that, if given tender loving care, Lilian—just like a flower—would spread joy and happiness all her life. Carlos wanted me to care for her in the same way he did. I agreed to do so, and, for some reason, he trusted me. I never got to know Lilian's mother too well, as she spoke mostly Spanish, and we were not able to communicate easily.

I want to take a moment to talk about Carlos. Carlos was happy doing little things that involved spending time, not money. Though he didn't have a lot of money, he lived a very rich life.

Rather than dining at the most expensive restaurants, he preferred patronizing a place in the mall or his favorite sandwich shop. He was always grateful for the food and enjoyed taking time to eat and talk. Carlos enjoyed going to bookstores and buying books; none of them were related to how to live comfortably after retirement or how to maximize your Social Security income. Rather, he enjoyed reading books about philosophy, history, and world religions. After retiring, he took up photography and art and bought books on how to take photos with a 35-millimeter camera, and on the French artist Matisse, whom he admired greatly.

Carlos went to church every Sunday. He knew I am a Hindu and told me every religion is preaching the same things, just differently; I understood what he meant. Carlos was passionate. He brought energy to many people who had more money than him but were depressed. Carlos was too busy to be depressed. He invested in *faith*.

Due to a decline in Elisa's health, she and Carlos moved to Asheville, North Carolina, where she later received 24/7 care at the Given's Estates health-care facility.

A few years later when Carlos visited us in Milwaukee, we took him to the Medical College of Wisconsin. Those were the burgeoning days of magnetic resonance imaging (MRI) research in the Biophysics Section of the Department of Radiology. We stopped by Radiology at Froedtert Hospital to show him the MRI facility. He started talking with Jim Hyde, director of the Biophysics Research Institute and a pioneer in MRI, and showed him a cyst on his wrist. Jim offered to arrange for MRI scanning and Carlos was pleased to see a beautiful MR image of his cyst. Although Carlos studied theology, he knew about clinical trials and their vital importance in making fundamental scientific discoveries to treat illness. He believed more people should participate in clinical trials in order to benefit humanity. It was not until many years after that evening that I realized the true significance of Carlos' words.

Duke Gardens is one of the most picturesque spots on the Duke University campus, and charges only a modest fee for weddings. In May of 1981, Reverend Carlos Alberto Rodriguez officiated our wedding at Duke Gardens. I wish my parents and family from India had been in attendance, but I was happy I had my friends from Alabama and North Carolina. Lilian's parents, sisters, brothers-in-law, and a few of their relatives and family friends attended our wedding. Lilian's college roommate, Deborah, was our maid of honor, and our flower girls were Lilian's nieces.

Our wedding, 1981.

It was a simple but memorable ceremony. We held our reception at the Pine Gate clubhouse next to the pool where we had met the year before. The wedding reception was a lot of fun, and everyone was in a great mood. Carlos was elated and giddy. Like me, if he thought something sounded funny, he would keep repeating it. Someone asked him for a church key, and he responded that he is a minister and does not need a church key. If you're not aware, a "church key" is a type of bottle or can opener. Monks would lock their beers in monastery cellars to keep them safe during the aging process; one story suggests that the term "church key" was used to refer to a certain type of bottle opener because it resembled the monks' keys. The use of the term was popularized by the brewing business.

Lilian and I arranged to go to Wrightsville Beach, east of Wilmington, North Carolina, for our honeymoon. We drove with our friend Mike and his girlfriend. I had reserved a block of rooms in a hotel near Johnnie Mercers Fishing Pier. When we arrived, we found that only one room was left for the four of us. Our friends from Alabama and North Carolina had arrived first and taken all the other rooms. Eventually, it all worked out, and Lilian and I had our own room.

Although Lilian was ready to move to Milwaukee with me for a couple of years, it was hard for her to leave North Carolina where she grew up. And it was difficult for me to leave the place where I spent three glorious years with friends and found happiness at work and in my life. The fond memories and lifelong friendships made during my time in "Chapel Thrill" are priceless.

Before Lilian and I moved to Milwaukee, her father presented me with a diary in which he had written everything he knew about Lilian; he asked me to read it during times of stress in our relationship and said that it would help guide us through the rough times. Carlos was an insightful man of great wisdom. He passed away just a few weeks before his ninety-seventh birthday.

I want to close out this chapter with a mention of Earl Marks, who was a very special person in our lives. Earl passed away in 2021—rest in peace, my friend!

Chapter 6

MILWAUKEE: A GREAT PLACE ON A GREAT LAKE

"My goal is to win in Milwaukee, bring a championship in the city, and make the team a lot better. So I would never leave for LA."
—Giannis "Greek Freak" Antetokounmpo

The Milwaukee Bucks beat the Phoenix Suns to win the National Basketball Association (NBA) championship in 2021. That year, Lilian surprised me with tickets to one of the playoff games in Milwaukee; it was exciting to watch Giannis Antetokounmpo and the team win, and then go on to compete for the championship! The last time the Bucks won the NBA championship was almost fifty years prior, when Kareem Abdul-Jabbar played for the team. After spending six years with the Bucks, Abdul-Jabbar was lured to play for the Los Angeles Lakers because of the city's more cosmopolitan atmosphere, diverse ethnicity, and culture.

Reportedly, he said the Bucks wouldn't get it done in game six against the Brooklyn Nets in the Eastern Conference finals in 2021, but Antetokounmpo and his teammates proved him wrong. The Fiserv Forum, a newly constructed multi-purpose sports and entertainment arena, became the home court of the Milwaukee Bucks in 2018. The area around it, known as the Deer District, is a premier location for sports, entertainment, and dining. Just south of the Deer District in downtown Milwaukee, renowned artist Mauricio Ramirez painted a three-story (fifty-six-foot) Giannis Antetokounmpo mural on the east side of the 600 East Building. Ramirez spent nearly 250 hours over a two-week period completing the painting. The 2021 Bucks were a dream team; many players—in addition to Antetokounmpo—were responsible for their championship win.

In the 1980s, when Lilian and I would check out new Milwaukee restaurants—like Edwardo's Pizza and City Club Downtown or Victor's on the East Side—we would see Sidney Moncrief, the late Bob Lanier, and other members of the Milwaukee Bucks. I became intrigued by the team. Don Nelson, one of the winningest coaches in NBA, was the Buck's coach for eleven years but had never won a championship. Often, the Bucks had phenomenal regular seasons; they were in several playoffs but never made it to the finals. A team has to be lucky to win it all in NBA. Now, Don Nelson is enjoying a relaxed life in Maui, Hawaii, playing poker with Willie Nelson. These two are a great pair indeed.

Milwaukee is known as Brew City because of the prominent beer brewing industry here and its long history with major beer companies, such as Miller and Pabst, and countless craft micro-breweries. It's also sometimes referred to as Cream City. This nickname is not related to the dairy industry abundant in the state of Wisconsin, nor the foamy head on a glass of beer; rather, it's because of the cream-colored bricks on many of the city's historic buildings.

Back in 1981, a few days after our Wrightsville Beach trip, Lilian and I were in our Toyota Corolla on our way to Milwaukee, Wisconsin. Lilian drove the entire fourteen hours from Chapel Hill because I did not know how to drive a stick shift. She was a trouper. After arriving in Milwaukee, we found an apartment in Wauwatosa (a suburb of Milwaukee) within walking distance of the Medical College of Wisconsin. It was so close, in fact, I could easily spot the college from our apartment. Lilian took a job working as a tax specialist at First Wisconsin Trust Company, which—at forty-two stories—remains the tallest building in downtown Milwaukee. Today, it is the iconic US Bank Center.

It was summer when we arrived in Milwaukee. We enjoyed spending time on the shore of Lake Michigan, at Bradford Beach on Lincoln Memorial Drive, and at the restaurant Pieces of Eight. Although the location was picturesque, with an extraordinary view of the city, the restaurant did not live up to its reputation. Several years ago, the restaurant closed and was replaced by an upscale seafood restaurant, Harbor House. According to Harbor House owner Joe Bartolotta, "Good seafood costs money and cheap seafood is not good."

Milwaukee skyline, 2022. Photo credit: Balaraman Kalyanaraman.

The Harbor House is nestled between the two architectural beauties: the Milwaukee Art Museum, referred to as "The Calatrava" by the locals, and Discovery World. The Calatrava was designed by Santiago Calatrava Valls, a Spanish architect, structural engineer, sculptor, and painter. The Quadracci Pavilion is the *pièce de résistance* of the Milwaukee Art Museum. The museum's signature wing-like sunscreen over the glass-enclosed Windhover Hall, the Burke Brise Soleil, has sensors that continually monitor wind speed and direction, closing the wings automatically when the wind speed is 23 mph or greater. According to Calatrava, the Quadracci Pavilion's design "responds to the culture of [Lake Michigan]: the sailboats, the weather, the sense of motion, and change."

On many weekends, we hung out with friends Lilian had made at work. We also joined a health and fitness club called Sea and Ski, located on 76th Street and Capitol Drive, where we met more friends: Roland, Jim and Mary, and Pat and JoAnne. Through Roland, we connected with many other friends. Then the health and fitness club became Club Universe. Lilian and I made fitness a priority and attended Club Universe every other day after work and on weekends.

After a few years at Club Universe, we were awarded the annual "Mr. and Mrs. Club Universe" title for our dedication to health and fitness. Club Universe eventually moved to a new location and some of us—Lilian and I, Roland, and Jim and Mary—decided to join Vic Tanny Health Club in Brookfield. We stayed on for many years after it changed to Bally Total Fitness. Following workouts at Bally's, we would go to the Bombay Bicycle Club, a popular Indian restaurant chain. After twenty years or so, Bally's closed and a few of us joined different clubs. Lilian and I joined Elite Sports Club. It was a good family-oriented fitness club and offered tennis lessons and other sports activities that our children enjoyed. I mainly went to do my forty-five-minute exercise routine followed by ten to fifteen minutes in the sauna;

it was no longer a social outing. We didn't have the same kind of comradery as we'd enjoyed previously. At the beginning of the COVID pandemic, we stopped going to the health club. Recently, we joined LifeTime Fitness. This is a totally different experience in working out. It's more like ScanTime Fitness! Everyone is glued to their smart phones during their workouts. I'm glad we spent more time talking with people between workouts, developing our interpersonal skills in the earlier days!

Since moving to Milwaukee, we have enjoyed the annual tradition of attending Summerfest, one of the world's largest music festivals, that takes place at Henry Maier Festival Park (also known as the Summerfest Grounds) on the Lake Michigan shore. Although the festival duration has changed in recent years, it used to run for eleven days, from noon until midnight, starting on the last Wednesday in June. The festival, which began in 1968, features both famous and upcoming musicians of various genres (including country, rock, alternative, jazz, blues, and many others) at different stages (Miller Lite Oasis, Harley Davidson Roadhouse, Briggs & Stratton Big Backyard, etc.). In recent years, some of these stage names have changed. We loved seeing Southern rock groups like Lynyrd Skynyrd, Gregg Allman Band, The Marshall Tucker Band, and The Charlie Daniels Band, to name a few. We have taken our friends from Tuscaloosa and Chapel Hill and visitors from other countries—including France, Germany, Poland, India, and England—to Summerfest.

Not only does Milwaukee have a professional basketball team, it is also home to a professional baseball team, the Milwaukee Brewers. Lilian and I attended numerous Brewers games at County Stadium. County Stadium was demolished in 2001, and Miller Park—which has since been renamed American Family Field—replaced it. We would go to the games with a big group of friends in several cars, which we would park next to one another for tailgate partying. This activity was new and interesting for us; it was amazing to see how well these parties were organized. For those unfamiliar with tailgating, like I was before living in Milwaukee, it is a major part of the sports ambience in the United States and Canada. Tailgate parties occur in the parking lots of stadiums. Friends grill out, share food, and consume enormous quantities of beverages prior to going into the stadiums to watch the games. As for me, I did not quite understand the game of baseball. I knew there was more to it than just hitting the ball out of the ballpark. As I mentioned in an earlier chapter, Robin Williams joked that cricket is baseball on Valium. In my opinion, baseball is like cricket on Valium *and* Lunesta. But the camaraderie of attending baseball games was a lot of fun. For many games, I spent most of my time in the parking lot, tailgating. Now, the rules have changed; tailgating must end thirty minutes after the game starts and fans are required to enter the ballpark or leave the premises.

The 1982 Brewers season was memorable. Particularly notable is the time I was outside Saz's State House, an iconic restaurant and sports bar in Milwaukee, waiting to catch the shuttle service to County Stadium before the World Series game against the St. Louis Cardinals. A lady was going around selling Brewers memorabilia (engraved plaques of Robin Yount and Paul Molitor, among other things) for fifteen dollars. These were collectors' items and could be valued at thousands of dollars in ten years, or so she told me. I said that I would wait to buy something the next year. She was prophetic and cautioned that the Brewers may not be in the World Series again in the next fifty years or even in my lifetime. The Brewers lost in the seventh game of the World Series (6–3) at the Busch Memorial Stadium, St. Louis, Missouri.

It turns out that, in the forty years that followed, the Brewers have not made it to the World Series again, although they came close to beating the Los Angeles Dodgers in the semifinals in 2021. The Brewers are one of six Major League Baseball teams that have never won a World Series. It was definitely a very big deal for the Brewers to get to the World Series in 1982. I'm amazed at how an ordinary person who was not an expert on the sport could be so right. It makes me think that the countless number of hours the talking heads spend before games is a total crock.

After moving to the Midwest, we embraced all four seasons, even the very cold, snowy one. Once, Lilian and I went cross-country skiing with our friends from her work. It was bone-chillingly cold and, even with hand warmers and gloves, our fingers were numb. In the beginning, a large group of us were on the trail together. The group slowly drifted apart, some skiing faster and others skiing slower, and became more spread out as we went along. Finally, only three of us—Lilian, Dave, and myself—were together. We later figured out that we were on a snowmobile trail, which explained why we saw so many snowmobiles. It was getting very late, and our fingers were nearly frozen. We could hear howling from afar. All I could think of was the latest hit from Duran Duran, "Hungry Like the Wolf." Dave and I were freaking out. We were planning how we would save Lilian in case a pack of wolves surrounded us. Lilian was cool-headed and thought we were being delirious. Finally, we found a bar. I was totally impressed to have found a bar on a snowmobile trail. Someone there told us that if we were on an actual cross-country trail, we would have found many more bars along the way. Well, chalk it up to experience!

Lilian took a job at United Community Center (UCC), located on the south side of Milwaukee in the heart of the Latino community. Her job involved grant writing, fundraising, and community development projects. We enjoyed participating in UCC events, and I especially liked going to UCC Café el Sol, a restaurant located in the Community Center that specializes in Mexican and Puerto Rican cuisine. On Fridays, there was live music performed by talented musicians from several Latin

American countries including Mexico, Puerto Rico, Peru, Columbia, and Cuba. Juan and Carmen became our good friends.

Juan and I went to the opening day of Summerfest for many years. We had a lot of fun. Come Hell or high water, we would not miss it. One year, whether we would attend was touch and go because Juan had his colonoscopy that morning. I called him around noon, while he was resting at home. Juan said he would not be able to make it because he was having a lot of stomach pain. I told him to lay on his stomach on the floor and lift his butt up. Juan did this and said he was feeling better within minutes; he also said he heard his old neighbors closing their windows and thought he probably had scared them off. Juan was ready for opening day!

Lilian, Door County, Wisconsin, 2022. Photo credit: Balaraman Kalyanaraman.

Lilian and I love traveling to Door County every October. Even during the COVID pandemic, we made the trip, taking all the necessary precautions. Door County is the peninsula between Green Bay, which is 100 miles north of Milwaukee, and Lake Michigan. It has miles and miles of shoreline, and many state parks and natural areas. It is ideal for outdoor recreation all year round, if you can tolerate the cold, snowy winters. If you enjoy scenic beauty, especially during autumn, the small-town lifestyle, the absence of chain restaurants, plentiful mom-and-pop shops, galleries, and quiet surroundings, then Door County is the place for you. A retirement advice magazine I read listed it among the best places to retire. About two million people visit Door County annually; we are among them.

Me in Door County, Wisconsin, 2022. Photo credit: Lilian Kalyanaraman.

Roland, Dave, and other friends would go to Upper Michigan ski resorts—Big Powderhorn Mountain Resort or Indian Head Resort—every winter. They would rent a couple of cottages, and we were invited to join them. Lilian had done some downhill skiing in college. But I had only seen this on TV. With Lilian's encouragement and help, I mustered enough courage to try it. It reminded me of an ice-skating adventure I had once in Chapel Hill. I got an A for effort and an F for execution. It was a miracle I didn't break any bones in my body (or in anyone else's body) during my kamikaze-style skiing. "Kamikaze" is a term used to define the Japanese suicide attacks in World War II. Not entirely unlike having several of those kamikaze drinks! Lilian used to say, "You pay for the entire slope. Why not use the whole slope?" When I complained of excruciating pain on my foot, our friend Gayle noticed that I had my boots on the wrong feet.

Then, my friends explained how to weight shift; that is a concept I am also trying to learn in golf. Since that time, we have skied in several places—Utah, Montana, Seattle, and even Chambery, an Alpine town in southeast France.

One day, after eight years of marriage, Lilian told me I was going to be a father. This was not a surprise, as we had planned to have a baby. I was happy but, until Regina was born, I did not realize how ecstatic I would be. Regina was so eager to get out into the world that she arrived more than three weeks early! Lilian was in labor for less than five hours, and Regina was born at 7:30 p.m. on a Friday. We were elated and amazed that we had brought this beautiful baby into the world.

Regina was a tiny baby, weighing five pounds and two ounces. She had to remain in the hospital until she gained a bit of weight. Also, her bilirubin levels were high, so the doctors were worried about jaundice. Baby Regina received phototherapy, which helped degrade the bilirubin, thus preventing liver damage. Every day we were notified of her blood bilirubin levels. After three days, I was convinced she was on the mend as the levels were decreasing linearly. It was a scare, but the doctors handled it as though it were routine. Baby Regina was a beautiful bundle of joy, and the best thing that could have happened to us.

Regina added a new dimension to our family, and we took her everywhere we went! She quickly adapted to our work routines, and at the age of two years, we enrolled her in Campus Child Care in Wauwatosa, where she learned her ABCs and quickly made friends. Growing up, she loved attending school. She received her bachelor's degree from the University of Wisconsin–Madison in four years with a high GPA. As of 2022, Regina is gainfully employed and in her first year of law school. We are very proud of her.

Since moving to Milwaukee, Lilian and I have done most things as a couple. There were a few things I did by myself. One of them was going out for dinner and a few drinks once a year with Roland, Steve, Zimmy, and Tom. I think Zimmy was the one who first referred to us as, or thought we looked like, the Rat Pack. It was delusional! Everyone in our age group has heard of the Rat Pack: Frank Sinatra, Dean Martin, Joey Bishop, Peter Lawford, and Sammy Davis Jr. Our tradition was that one of the Rat Pack members would pick me up, and we'd start the evening at a supper club (Coerper's Five O'Clock Steakhouse) followed by visits to a few downtown nightspots. By the end of the evening, we probably looked like a pack of rats. The next morning, Lilian would ask me, "How is your headache?" I could only do that once a year! Sadly, Tom passed away in 2022. RIP!

Another annual tradition was to participate in a golf outing. Although I was more of a hacker than a golfer, I was happy to be a part of a foursome in the Golf Fore Wolfe fundraising event for ten or more years. The rest of my team consisted of good golfers, Roland, Jerry, and Rick. Usually, this was my only golf outing, so a few months before I would try to practice in my yard. The golf outing was a best ball scramble, and although my tee shots usually did not go very far, the other guys were good at launching theirs way down the fairway. Greg Norman said that golf is 30% long game and 70% short game. Also, the pros say that you swing for the show and putt for the dough. So, I would try to contribute a little by practicing my approach shots and my pitching wedge.

This fundraising event started many years ago in memory of Eric Wolfe who loved golf and used to say, "It's always a great day for golf." Eric was a graduate student at the University of Wisconsin–Madison. Sadly, Eric was diagnosed with brain cancer when he was twenty-three years old. After treatment with radiation and chemotherapy at the University of Wisconsin–Madison Carbone Cancer Center, he lived for five more years.

His parents, Jerry and Nancy Wolfe, started an annual golf outing to raise money for brain tumor research, specifically for the Eric Wolfe Brain Tumor Professorship. The proceeds from this event already have made a difference in the treatment of brain tumors. A couple of the discoveries made possible by the Wolfe Professorship include the use of targeted radiation treatment such that the healthy tissue surrounding the tumor is spared, and delivery of pulsed low-dose radiation in relapsed brain tumors. More than ten years after the death of his son, Jerry is ready to let go of the past and move on. The positive energy he infused into this event will keep it going for many years to come. It is likely that new discoveries in brain cancer diagnoses and treatments will increase survival rates in patients with brain cancer.

One of the highlights of Lilian's and my life together was our daughter, Regina's, wedding, where she married Scott. Lilian did a wonderful job with the wedding planning. The event brought together my and Lilian's relatives, who met for the first time ever. It was a great gathering that accentuated both of our cultures and showed that we had managed to mesh our cultural differences with our similarities. The wedding ceremony and reception took place at Renaissance Place in Milwaukee, designed by American architect Solon Spencer Beman. The building had been a church and was renovated to maintain its original design, while accommodating contemporary needs. I know in most American wedding receptions, the focus is on the open bar, and free beer and wine, rather than on the food. Generally, the food is more of a filler. Lilian knew I am particular about food. She had the food catered by Zilli Hospitality Group, which creatively caters many different types of cuisine, including Indian; it was a big hit. The disk jockey was clever enough to adapt to us and played Bollywood dance songs. I heard someone say after the wedding, "I have attended a lot of Wisconsin weddings, but this one was the most fun."

Lilian and I celebrated our fortieth wedding anniversary in May 2021, in Miami. It was a warm, romantic evening as we walked along the beach together, under a gorgeous full moon; it seems appropriate that the "moon over Miami" coincided with our forty years of marriage. I believe you get out what you put into any relationship. Respect, trust, and civility are some of the ingredients that are essential to a sustainable relationship. As a rabbi once said, "You cannot get a prescription for a happy and lasting relationship. Everyone must write their own prescription that changes with time; as we grow older, we invariably grow apart or become interested in other things." Everything around us changes with time. Our relationships change as well. I read somewhere that marriage is like a deck of cards. In the beginning, all you need is two hearts and a diamond. By the end, you wish you had a club and a spade. But it does not have to be that way. As the rabbi said, *change your prescription.* Why not wish for a king of hearts and a queen of diamonds or a king of diamonds and a queen of hearts?

After having spent a few years in Milwaukee, we felt moving away from Chapel Hill was one of the best decisions we could have made. In Milwaukee, we met mutual acquaintances who became our good friends. We learned to have good communication and participate together in shared interests and activities; these have all been vital to our long-lasting relationship.

Chapter 7
BECOMING A CHEESEHEAD

"Reggie, this is God. Come to Green Bay."
—Mike Holmgren

"Green Bay's always been an underdog. Coaches would tell a player, 'If you don't get your act together, we're going to ship you to Green Bay' . . . I think every team was shocked I picked Green Bay."
—Reggie White

Story has it that Mike Holmgren, former head coach of the Green Bay Packers, imitated God to lure Reggie White to play for the Packers. At least, that is part of the story. Ron Wolf, general manager of the Packers at that time, knew the Packers needed a massive turnaround with high-powered, high-caliber recruits in order to become a championship-level team. More importantly, he knew he needed to revamp the defense. Wolf wanted someone who would change the culture in Green Bay, and he had White—one of the best defensive ends—in mind. The Packers had already signed Brett Favre, who had been with the Atlanta Falcons the prior year. Favre was the quarterback for the Southern Mississippi Golden Eagles in 1990 when they beat the Alabama Crimson Tide during Gene Stallings' debut as head coach of Alabama.

Cheesehead from India, 2022. Photo credit: Lilian Kalyanaraman.

Holmgren and Packers Defensive Coordinator Ray Rhodes went to Knoxville, Tennessee, to have lunch with White's family. White was deeply religious and often said it was not up to him to decide what he wants to do in the future, it was up to God. A few days later, Holmgren allegedly left a message on White's answering machine, "Reggie, this is God. Come to Green Bay." As we all know, White became a Packer, and the team went from being twenty-third in defense to winning the Super Bowl.

The 1996 Green Bay Packers season was magical. The Packers had the National Football League's (NFL) highest-scoring offense and allowed the fewest points on defense. Green Bay finished the season with number-one ranked offense, defense, and special teams. The Packers were undefeated at home. Holmgren and Favre were close; Holmgren referred to Favre as the son he never had.

You know you are a cheesehead when your life revolves around the Packers. It was happening to me; I became a naturalized cheesehead. My schedule during football season was largely dependent on when the Packers played. This is true for most cheeseheads in Wisconsin and was true for this cheesehead even when I was 7,000 miles away from Wisconsin.

I still remember the divisional playoff game when Green Bay finally beat San Francisco. I was in Chennai, India, at that time.

Just like people remember a newsworthy event such as Neil Armstrong landing on the moon or the assassination of John F. Kennedy and recall where they were when it happened, I remember most of the big games that Green Bay played starting in the 1980s. This is a typical cheesehead thing.

In January 1996, I was staying with my sister and my brother-in-law, who was a huge sports fan. He loved cricket, tennis, and soccer, so he had all the sports channels. The Packer/San Francisco 49ers game came on around 2:00 a.m. on a Monday morning, as the time difference between San Francisco and Chennai is about thirteen hours. I was up most of the night; the TV was in the living room, and I did not want to wake anyone up, so I kept the volume low. As the game went on, I could not contain my excitement. I was so wired that I was high fiving the wall. This woke up my brother-in-law, who came downstairs. He was surprised to see me in this state and asked what was happening. Most people in India do not know or care about the NFL, but my brother-in-law and my sister regularly visited Chicago, so he was familiar with the Chicago Bears. I explained the winner of next week's game would be in the Super Bowl, and that the game would be played in Green Bay, giving the Packers the home-field advantage. I was an ecstatic cheesehead.

I returned to Milwaukee a few days before the next game. Lilian and I hosted a party at our home to watch the Packers play the Carolina Panthers at Lambeau Field in the National Football Conference (NFC) Championship game. This party was particularly memorable because one of our friends, another enthusiastic cheesehead, said he would run around the block in his underwear every time the Packers scored. The Packers won 30–13, so he did this many times, even though it was a frigid day with a windchill around -10°F.

The Packers went on to beat the New England Patriots (35–21) at Super Bowl XXXI to win their third Vince Lombardi Trophy. Desmond Howard's ninety-nine-yard kickoff return for a touchdown was the longest in Super Bowl history. He was also the first player on special teams to win the Super Bowl Most Valuable Player award. The sight of Favre jubilantly running down the field of the Superdome after the win was unforgettable! Only true cheeseheads would remember these things.

On January 11, 2004, I was in Mumbai visiting my brother during another playoff game between Green Bay and the Philadelphia Eagles, at Lincoln Financial Field in Philadelphia, Pennsylvania. Lilian held a Packer party at our place. I had asked her to call me—no matter that it would be around 5:00 a.m. the next morning in Mumbai—if the Packers won. When I did not receive a call from Lilian, I knew the Packers had lost the game. What does "fourth and twenty-six" mean in football? It refers to the play that happened during the fourth quarter, with Packers leading the Eagles 17–14. The time remaining was one minute and twelve seconds, with no timeouts available. The Eagles faced a fourth-down situation from their own twenty-five-yard line. They needed twenty-six yards to convert for a first down. If

Green Bay stopped them, it was game over. Donovan McNabb threw a perfect strike to wide receiver Freddie Mitchell, who was brought down at Green Bay's forty-six-yard line, and the subsequent plays set up a field goal that was good. The game went into overtime, then sudden-death overtime. Favre threw an interception that set up another field goal, giving the Eagles a 20–17 victory. I did not feel good the next day. When my brother asked me if something was wrong, I told him I had a bit of a headache. Actually, I had a Packers (not alcohol)-induced hangover, something many cheeseheads can relate to!

I was invited to speak at a symposium on oxidative stress in Bangalore (now known as Bengaluru), India. The symposium was the day before the January 9, 2005, wild-card game between the Packers and the Minnesota Vikings. My lecture was at 10:00 a.m., and the game was probably over around 9:00 a.m. Bangalore time. I did not want to know the outcome—Packers win or loss—before my talk, as I did not want any distraction. After my presentation, I got a phone call from Srigiridhar "Giri" Kotamraju, a former postdoctoral fellow in my lab at the Medical College of Wisconsin. Giri said the Vikings had won 31–17 and mentioned a controversial move by the Vikings' wide receiver, Randy Moss: After a touchdown reception, Moss mooned the Packers fans. Cris Collinsworth, the color commentator, took it in stride and seemed to think it was funny that Moss "shot the moon" (or, rather, he eclipsed it). But the play-by-play commentator, Joe Buck, did not have the same sense of humor. He said it was a "disgusting act" that had unfortunately aired live. Yeah, this was one of those "come on, man" moments. Moss only pretended to moon the fans; it was all in jest. Moss was fined $10,000.

In 1997, the year after the Packers won the Vince Lombardi Trophy, they became the leading contender in the NFL. The Packers finished the regular season with a 13–3 record and won their second consecutive NFC Championship, again beating the 49ers but this time at Lambeau Field. Lambeau Field is nicknamed the “Frozen Tundra.” It’s an outdoor stadium, and winter football games played there are notoriously frigid, so calling it a “treeless plain of arctic regions having a permanently frozen layer below the surface of the soil” seems fitting. However, the Frozen Tundra nickname became notorious after the December 31, 1967, Ice Bowl game between the Packers and the Dallas Cowboys, when the temperature fell to -18°F with wind chills as low as -48°F—the second coldest NFL game on record. The electric heating system that had been installed earlier in the season proved faulty, and condensation that had formed under the tarp before the game had turned to ice. John Facenda, an American sports announcer known to fans as the “Voice of God,” has often been miscredited with being the first to refer to Lambeau Field as the Frozen Tundra. A debatable piece of cheesehead trivia!

The Packers played the Denver Broncos in Super Bowl XXXII on January 25, 1998, in San Diego, California. Once again, Lilian and I had organized a Packer party at our home. We made all the preparations for the party, and everything was set. We were happily awaiting our second child, as Lilian was due any day that week, so we knew our plans would be “touch-and-go.” The day before the Packer party, I took Regina to see the new Spice Girls movie; she was a big fan.

Later that night, Lilian went into labor, so we drove to the hospital. Lilian’s doctor, Dr. Cruikshank, said, “It looks like you’re going to have a Super Bowl baby.” As he predicted, our son, Rajiv, was born on Super Bowl Sunday, weighing seven pounds and four ounces. Mom and baby were doing well, and we were excited to welcome our newest bundle of joy to the family. It was a great day! I called my friends, who were happy for us, and expressed their understanding that the party would probably be canceled. But I did the worst thing a cheesehead could do; I had the party anyway! Some people showed up and, of course, we all talked about Lilian and baby Rajiv, and how we missed them. The Broncos defeated the Packers, 31–24. Lilian was a trouper and forgave me for having the Packer party. I really was a dumbass cheesehead!

Rajiv didn't like the Broncos for a long time because he had heard the story of his birth too often. Rajiv went to Eisenhower for elementary school, Brookfield Academy for middle school, and Wauwatosa West for high school; he enjoyed playing soccer from the age of four years through college. Rajiv attended Marquette University College of Business and graduated in four years. As of 2022, he is working and taking Master of Business Administration courses at the University of Wisconsin–Milwaukee. We are very proud of Rajiv!

That Super Bowl loss marked the end of the Holmgren era. He moved on to become manager and coach of the Seattle Seahawks. Reggie White's era in Green Bay also ended, and he went to play for the Carolina Panthers. Brett Favre was traded to the New York Jets, thus beginning the era of Aaron Rodgers, who had been waiting in the wings for a long time. The Packers had to regroup their offense and defense.

With Mike McCarthy as the head coach, the 2010 Packers season was a miracle. They finished the season with a 9–7 record, and actually made it to the playoffs! As Jim Mora, head coach of the Indianapolis Colts once famously said, "Playoffs? Are you kidding me? Playoffs?!" With that record? The mindset of the Packers team was different—records didn't matter; what really mattered was the intensity with which the game was played. The road to the Super Bowl meant that the Packers had to win three playoff games, and they would not have the home-field advantage for any of them.

The Packers beat the Eagles 21–16 in the first round. Of course, everyone was acutely aware of the fourth down completion of twenty-six yards by McNabb in Philadelphia (i.e., the 4–26 debacle), but the chemistry was right this time around. The second game was in Atlanta against the Falcons. The Falcons were formidable, and no one thought the Packers had a chance of winning. Rodgers orchestrated the offense like a seasoned symphony conductor; every facet of the game was in perfect harmony. Rodgers had the finest receiving squad in Jordy Nelson, Greg Jennings, Donald Driver, and James Jones, and running backs James Starks and John Kuhn. And Charles Woodson, Clay Matthews, and the rest of the defensive squad caused four Atlanta turnovers. Final score: Green Bay 48, Atlanta 21. We had hosted another Packer party at our house, and in the middle of the game, the phone rang. I don't know why, but I rushed to the kitchen to answer it. Allen Cowley, chair of the Department of Physiology, was on the line; he never called me at home. My friends were screaming that I was missing a Packers touchdown. I told Allen that it better be important. Allen apologized for calling during the Packers game; he was unaware I'd become a cheesehead since moving to Wisconsin. Of course, Allen was doing what he had been asked to do—let all the basic science chairs know that the dean of the Medical College of Wisconsin had been let go. When I got off the phone, I went right back to watching the game, but I regretted having missed the touchdown, as cheeseheads never miss a Packers touchdown.

The season's NFC championship game was against the Chicago Bears at Soldier Field in Chicago, Illinois. It was cold. The solid defense of Green Bay helped them prevail over the Bears. B. J. Raji (aka "The Freezer") made his debut interception and return for a touchdown, which helped the Packers seal the deal. Sam Shields had two picks. Final score: Chicago 14, Green Bay 21.

The Packers advanced to the Super Bowl XLV to play the Pittsburgh Steelers on February 6, 2011, at the Cowboys Stadium in Arlington, Texas. It was a classic game with two iconic quarterbacks: Ben Roethlisberger and Aaron Rodgers. The Packers' defense stopped the final drive of the game. Green Bay defeated Pittsburgh, 31–25, and the most valuable player of the game was Rodgers. The Packers were the first six-seed team in the NFC to win the Super Bowl. The halftime show featured performances by the Black Eyed Peas, Usher, and Slash.

Cheeseheads love to rehash the Packers games, regardless of whether they win or lose. My Monday lunches with Peter Newman, Deb Newman, Jim Hyde, Karen Hyde, Joy Joseph, and Bill O'Brien were always fun. We would analyze every aspect of Packer games. We kept having to find a bigger table for lunch, as more people gravitated to join us. One of the department chairs told me he was envious of us having such a great time during the middle of the day. In addition to sports, our conversations covered science, the stock market, movies, politics, physical ailment . . . you name it, we discussed it.

In 2009, Favre was traded from the New York Jets to the Minnesota Vikings—something the Packers organization had avoided at all costs when trading Favre the previous year. Favre played only one season in Minnesota, and it was one of the best season-long performances of his career. The Vikings were 12–4. He took them to the NFC Championship game against the New Orleans Saints, held in the Superdome. It was a sloppy game with lots of turnovers on both sides. With a minute or so left, the game was tied, and the Vikings had the ball on the Saints' thirty-three-yard line. It was a fifty-yard field goal within Ryan Longwell's reach. Twelve men in the huddle? Who's counting? To quote radio announcer, and Vikings fan, Paul Allen: "Brett Favre goes back to pass, he pumps, now he fires over the middle. Intercepted . . . You've got to be kidding me; I can't believe what I just saw . . . But why do you even ponder passing? I mean, you can take a knee and try a fifty-six-yard field goal. This is not Detroit, man! This is the Super Bowl." The

Gunslinger (as Favre was nicknamed) had recklessly passed the ball. He was doing his best to win the game during regulation.

As one sports analyst said later, "Brett Favre did not lose the game. It was the poor coaching by the Vikings."

Believe it or not, I was rooting against Brett Favre. I was not the only one; I think most of Packer Nation wanted to see him fail. In any case, it is one thing to root against the Vikings, but to root against Favre—who had thrilled us a countless number of Sunday afternoons—seemed reprehensible. Every Packer fan remembers the awe-inspiring Monday night game the day after Favre's father passed away; Favre threw for 399 yards and four touchdowns to beat the Raiders 41–7. I did not like the person I had become; I was an ugly cheesehead.

After a Packer loss, cheeseheads all over the globe are devastated. How could the Packers lose consecutive NFC playoff games (Tampa Bay and San Francisco) at the Frozen Tundra in January? Pondering the answers to questions like this causes cheeseheads a tremendous amount of angst. But, football- and sports-related happiness is transient, especially at the professional level where the games are all business. Philosophically speaking, I finally realized football is just a game, and whichever team plays with more intensity and desire, with a little luck, will win. I let Lilian know I was no longer going to lose any sleep over the Packers or the associated drama; I didn't need to experience the roller coaster of emotions over which players will stay and which will leave (e.g., Rodgers in 2021 and 2022) that cheeseheads have no control over.

One evening recently, when Lilian and I were returning home after shopping, she asked if I wanted to watch a movie. I told her I'd rather see what happens in the 2022 NFL Draft; the Packers had two first-round picks. Lilian was in disbelief, as she thought I had overcome my Packers addiction. I was already feeling hopeful for the 2022 season. Defense wins championships. Remember Reggie White, Santana Dotson, Clay Matthews, A. J. Hawk, Charles Woodson? The Packers' two first-round draft picks were defensive players from the Georgia Bulldogs; this could change the Packers' defensive landscape over the next few years.

Cheeseheads never die—they simply fade away.

Chapter 8

THE MEDICAL COLLEGE OF WISCONSIN: KNOWLEDGE CHANGING LIFE (1981 TO DATE)

"The only way to do great work is to love what you do." —
Steve Jobs

"It takes twenty years to build a reputation
and five minutes to ruin it.
If you think about that, you'll do things differently."
—Warren Buffet

If you do what you love, you will never work a day in your life (Marc Anthony gets credit for this quote). Tim Cook, who succeeded Steve Jobs as CEO of Apple, disagrees with that statement. In fact, he thinks it is a "total crock." His stance is that when you find a job you love, you will work harder than before because you don't mind doing so and if you work for money and money alone, you will never be happy. All these motivational messages should be taken with a grain of sodium chloride (also known as common salt). Who is going to argue with Tim Cook? The market cap of Apple went up almost eight times from $350 billion to $3 trillion[3] since Cook took over.

The bottom line is that you should love what you do, work hard and smart, and—whenever feasible—create your own trail and ideas while maintaining the oft-quoted "work-life balance" every day. I strongly believe everyone's job is important and significant, and everyone can innovate and create in any job; innovation is not reserved for the few people at the top. If all employees are aligned in the same direction, the mindset and culture of an institution will change with a positive synergy. When this happens, the ranking of the institution will increase. Another motto that is applicable to every profession, including scientific research, is the one uttered by Warren Buffet (included as an epigraph to this chapter). I often tell others—and frequently remind myself—that the most important currency we have in our profession is scientific integrity, and there are no shortcuts in science.

When I arrived at the Medical College of Wisconsin (MCW) in 1981, the Biophysics Section was part of the Department of Radiology, chaired by Jim Youker. Years earlier, Harold "Hal" Swartz, recruited to MCW Radiology, wanted to establish the Electronic Spin Resonance facility, which later became the National Biomedical EPR Center, or EPR Center for short. Hal was interested in studying radiation-induced effects in tissues and the role of free radicals in cancers. As discussed previously, electron paramagnetic resonance (EPR) is the only technique that can unambiguously detect and identify the structure of free radicals.

3) Apple briefly hit a market cap of $3 trillion on January 3, 2022 (Lewsing 2022).

In 1975, Hal convinced Jim Hyde from Varian Associates in Palo Alto, California, specializing in nuclear magnetic resonance and EPR technology, to move to MCW. Jim and Hal became co-directors of the Biophysics Section. Bringing Jim Hyde to MCW was a visionary move on the part of Hal, Jim Youker, and Jerry Scanlon. As everyone knows now, Jim Hyde transformed the magnetic resonance research landscape here, and MCW became one of the premier research institutions in EPR and MRI, both nationally and internationally. Jim Hyde also had the most outstanding skill in identifying and recruiting smart, talented people. Now, search firms specialize in finding people with talent for different jobs, but in those days, word of mouth played a huge role. Jim Hyde, the pioneer, leader, and icon in magnetic resonance research, passed away in August 2022. I had the honor and privilege of giving the eulogy at his funeral.

A friend and former classmate of mine, Sridhar C. N., from the Indian Institute of Technology in Bombay was working at Marquette University's Chemistry Department. Three years after I joined MCW, he called to tell me that he'd run into a very interesting Polish guy, Andrzej Jesmanowicz, who was working at the Sony TV repair store near Mayfair Mall in Wauwatosa.

He said that Andrzej was a genius who could diagnose and fix a problem that no other TV repair person could. Andrzej had told Sridhar his life story; he had earned a PhD in physics from Copernicus University in Poland and had received postdoctoral training at the University of Windsor in Ontario, Canada, and the Fritz-Haber-Institute in West Berlin, Germany. Andrzej was also very much involved in the Solidarity Movement in Poland in the early 1980s. Solidarity, the first trade union created in Poland and led by Lech Walesa, was an anti-Communist government movement to further workers' rights and social change. The Solidarity movement was banned through the imposition of martial law, but in the end, it succeeded in helping to overthrow Communism in

Poland. During this period, Andrzej and his family had to leave Poland. Andrzej was interested in EPR technology, so Sridhar told him about the EPR Center at MCW.

The next day, Andrzej called me, and I invited him to come over to the EPR Center. I took him to Jim Hyde's office and introduced them. Jim reluctantly agreed to chat with Andrzej. I did not see Andrzej most of the day and later found out that Jim had offered him a job. Andrzej came to my office to thank me, although I had not done anything. Andrzej changed everything in the EPR Center. People had a hard time figuring out what he was talking about, although they understood everything he said. Andrzej was loud, but the signal to noise was maximal. Jim and Andrzej obtained many patents, and together they made innovative discoveries not only in EPR, but also in MRI/functional MRI technology at MCW. In his free time, Andrzej enjoyed skydiving, helped make movies of skydiving during formation, and even figured out how to prevent goggles from fogging during skydiving. Andrzej was an outstanding scientist, creative thinker, and wonderful human being, and our memories of him will be with us forever.

I was working with Roger Sealy, who was co-director of the EPR Center. As a postdoctoral research associate, I did not have to worry about anything except doing the work. I shared an office with various visiting scientists who rotated through Biophysics, including Tom Grist (now chair of the Department of Radiology at the University of Wisconsin–Madison). Once I had the pleasure of sharing the office with Professor Stanislaw Lukiewicz from the Jagiellonian University (established in 1364) in Krakow, Poland. When I addressed him as Stan, he told me that he preferred to be called Professor Lukiewicz. I apologized to him, and since that time it was always Professor Lukiewicz for me. Professor Lukiewicz was responsible for initiating the collaboration between the Jagiellonian University and MCW that began in 1979. Professor Lukiewicz had told Jim Hyde that highly talented physicists with expertise in EPR worked in his department in Krakow, and that it would be mutually beneficial to start a visiting scientist program at MCW. Those were the days of the Cold War, and it was not easy to travel back and forth between the United States and Poland or other Eastern European countries. The visiting scientist program was a game changer; the collaborations between Jim and Wojciech Froncisz led to new discoveries that fundamentally transformed the application of EPR technology in biological studies. Tadeusz "Tad" Sarna initiated a collaboration on melanin research with Roger Sealy and Jim. Melanins are pigmented, polymeric molecules present in the skin, eye, and even brain. At that time, EPR was the only technique that could provide biophysical and biochemical information on melanins. The National Institutes of Health (NIH) awarded a grant to Jim and Hal (as principal investigators) to examine the structure and function of melanins; Roger was a co-investigator on the grant.

In 1989, the first in a series of EPR workshops on the Applications of EPR in Biology and Medicine was held in Krakow. The workshops were a collaborative effort between MCW and the Jagiellonian University that have resulted in hundreds of scientific publications, and the recruitment of graduate students, postdoctoral fellows, and visiting professors to MCW. These workshops were held every two to three years, and the first five were alternately organized by W. Karol Subczynski, Professor Lukiewicz, and Tad. After I became the chair of Biophysics at MCW, Tad, Wojciech, and I organized the sixth EPR workshop for the new Faculty of Biochemistry, Biophysics and Biotechnology at the Jagiellonian University. When I saw Professor Lukiewicz in Krakow, I said, "Good morning, Professor Lukiewicz." He said, "Call me Stan." In his mind, I'd earned the right to call him by his first name. I was pleased. Sadly, that was the last time I saw Professor Lukiewicz before he passed away. Tad and I organized the next four workshops in Krakow, two of them with Wolfgang Lubitz from the Max Planck Institute for Chemical Energy Conversion and Bruce Freeman from the University of Pittsburgh. These workshops attracted scientists from Russia, Germany, the United Kingdom, France, Italy, Israel, India, Japan, Croatia, Denmark, Australia, Bulgaria, the United States, and Poland. The scientific collaboration between MCW and the Jagiellonian University has spanned more than four decades.

In the initial stages, most of my work with Roger was focused on understanding the biophysical and biochemical properties of melanins. Roger started a productive collaboration with Arvind Menon, a melanin researcher from the University of Toronto, Canada. We investigated the sun-protective and sun-damaging effects of melanin pigments. We made several key discoveries showing that ultraviolet light could induce formation of hydrated electrons from melanin pigment and other oxidants formed from oxygen. Our work also revealed key mechanistic differences in ultraviolet-induced oxidation of eumelanin (black pigment) and pheomelanin (red pigment) that could explain the enhanced susceptibility of red-haired, fair-skinned individuals to cancer from sunlight exposure. This was a fascinating area of research that impacted our understanding of many skin conditions such as psoriasis, vitiligo, and hyperpigmentation.

Once, I consulted a dermatologist about hyperpigmentation. To treat it, the dermatologist instructed me to carefully rub a lotion on the affected area on my face. I asked the dermatologist whether the lotion would inhibit the enzyme, tyrosinase, in melanocytes (i.e., skin cells producing the melanin). I found out that one of the lotion's major components is the chemical, hydroquinone, which is a competitive inhibitor of the enzyme, tyrosinase. The actual mechanism still is not fully understood but use of hydroquinone comes with the risk of bleaching the non-hyperpigmented areas of the skin. Science won over vanity in this case, and I chose not to go through with the treatment. Many autoimmune skin conditions are related to insufficient or lack of melanin formation.

In his role serving on MCW's admissions committee, Roger interviewed many potential students and was skillful in evaluating people. He became interested in psychology. When Roger decided to pursue a psychology career, he said he would transfer his grants to me after obtaining permission from MCW and the NIH. A pre-requisite to serving in the role of principal investigator on NIH grants is to have a faculty position, so I was promoted to the rank of assistant professor in the Department of Radiology in 1984.

Roger was a great scientist and a great human being. He also was instrumental in helping me obtain my green card, which is the immigrant visa that allows for permanent residence in the United States. I had a J-1 visa when I was working at the NIEHS. One of the conditions of this visiting scientist program was that I would have to go back to India for two years before I could apply for permanent residency. This caused a lot of strain. Lilian was incredibly understanding of the situation; we spent thousands of dollars in attorney fees fighting to obtain a waiver of this two-year foreign residency, but nothing worked. The offices of Wisconsin Senator William Proxmire and US House Representative Jim Moody even tried to help my cause, but to no avail. The only route for me to avoid the program's conditions was to get a waiver from the NIH, which was offered based on the outstanding scientific credentials of the applicant and their potential contributions to advancing science in the United States. Roger was aware of my problem and was willing to be a sponsor; he obtained recommendation letters from other renowned scientists in the United States on my behalf. Without his help, I don't think I would ever have received letters like that. I was truly humbled. We were elated when the NIH finally granted me the waiver, something that everyone told me had a 1% chance of success.

When Roger left MCW, someone said that the field of psychology needed him more. We kept in touch for a while; he moved on, and I became immersed in the world of science research, trying to fill his shoes. Tad and I continued working on melanin, but it became clear that for me to compete for grants, I needed to collaborate with someone in the United States who had expertise in pigment cell biology. When I could not find a suitable collaborator, I decided to work on alternate but related research projects.

At the time, Kent Kirk, professor of microbiology at the University of Wisconsin–Madison and a National Academy of Sciences member, was leading a group at the USDA Forest Products Lab involved in investigating lignin degradation. The intracellular pH of rotting wood is very low and an enzyme, lignin peroxidase, responsible for formation of lignin polymer also caused its degradation under certain conditions. One of Kent's postdoctoral fellows called me to do EPR analyses to figure out the mechanism. We worked with lignin model compounds, and our work revealed new mechanistic information. One of the key findings was the carbon-carbon bond breakage initiated by the activated lignin peroxidase enzyme. Kent told me some of these findings would be published in a microbiology textbook on lignin degradation. Subsequent collaborations with this group showed how this enzyme helps in the degradation and detoxication of recalcitrant environmental chemicals such as TCDD (2,3,7,8-tetrachlorodibenzo para dioxin) and polycyclic aromatic hydrocarbons. It was an exciting and productive collaboration.

I became interested in photochemistry and photobiology research. Larry Hopwood, director of the Radiation Biology Section of the Department of Radiation Oncology at MCW headed by Frank Wilson, suggested that I contact Fritz Sieber who had joined MCW. Fritz was interested in the antileukemic mechanism of merocyanine dye. He was using this dye (called merocyanine

540 or MC-540) and visible light from fluorescent lamps. This modality of killing tumor cells with a dye and visible light in the presence of oxygen is known as photodynamic therapy. I decided to study the mechanism of action of MC-540. I had experimental proof that MC-540 generates a toxic species called singlet oxygen that reacts with lipids, proteins, and even DNA to cause modifications that are toxic to cells. Since the dye selectively binds to leukemic cells and not to normal cells, MC-540 is selectively toxic to cancer cells and spares the normal cells—a very desirable and essential property for a potential antitumor drug. We compiled a group—consisting of Albert "Al" Girotti, Jimmy Feix, Fritz, and me—to submit a program project grant studying the biophysical, biochemical, cell biological, and clinical applications of MC-540 phototherapy for leukemia. With Al as the overall principal investigator, we received the first—and only—program project grant awarded to MCW from the National Cancer Institute (NCI).

That was a great achievement. Again, Larry helped start this project. Our combined expertise generated an impactful paper that was published in the *Proceedings of the National Academy of Sciences, USA (PNAS)*. Results showed that oxygen is converted to a reactive oxygen species during light activation of MC-540 and reacts with the membranes of cancer cells to form toxic products that kill the cells. Ravinder Jit Singh, who is now the director of Mayo Clinic Endocrine Laboratory, did a lot of work with MC-540 in membranes while he was a postdoctoral fellow in my lab. Fritz was collaborating with Neal Flomenberg, a pediatric clinician, on the project.

Patients' bone marrow tissues were removed, mixed with MC-540, and irradiated with light from fluorescent lamps; then, the bone marrow tissues were transfused back to the patients. This was known as leukemic cell purging of bone marrow. This type of therapy was less toxic and showed impressive results in shrinking the tumors. When Flomenberg left MCW, the clinical arm of the project was disabled. Although we renewed the program project grant for three more years, we could not continue without the clinical collaboration. During this period, we generated many fundamentally important photochemical/photobiological concepts that could be used by future photodynamic therapy researchers. Once again, I found myself looking for a medically relevant project where my expertise in basic science would be a good fit.

In my PhD research, I had investigated free radical formation in single crystals after radiation at low temperatures (liquid nitrogen). That expertise became useful in studying real life tissues. As most of you know by now, I am an avid reader of scientific articles, especially those centered on free radicals in biological systems. I became aware of a paper in a prestigious journal published by a group of researchers from a top-ranking US medical school. This work was centered on free radical production formed during ischemia and reperfusion injury to the heart. I did not agree with the interpretations in that paper, even though the work received accolades at American Heart Association meetings and in high-impact journals. My friend and mentor, Irwin Fridovich, told me he does not correct a mistake or flaw in a paper unless others use the paper in support of their work, resulting in propagation of the mistake. What he meant was that a mistake such as this should be corrected. I decided to correct the paper on ischemia and reperfusion. I collaborated with John Baker, a cardiothoracic surgery researcher at MCW. John came from St. Thomas' Hospital Medical School in London where he worked under the direction of David Hearse. Incidentally, David Hearse was first to coin the phrase "reperfusion injury" or reperfusion-induced injury. During heart bypass surgery, the blood supply is stopped briefly; this condition lacking oxygen is called ischemia, and when the oxygen supply is resumed, the ischemic tissues undergo damage, which is called reperfusion injury. This type of injury to tissues was also observed in organ transplant studies. John had great expertise in isolated rat heart studies that mimicked the ischemia-reperfusion injury. Eugene Konorov from the Cardiology Research Center in Moscow joined my group as a postdoctoral fellow. Eugene's expertise was in cardiovascular pharmacology, and he began collaborating with John and me on this project. We monitored free radical production in isolated rat hearts after cardioplegic ischemia and reperfusion. Our work revealed the artifacts of the previous work, and our rebuttal was published in the *PNAS* journal. We received an NIH grant and made important contributions to the understanding of cardioprotection during cardioplegic ischemia and reperfusion. My only regret is that we did not patent our cardioplegic solution containing novel cardioprotective agents. The existing mixtures (Carolina rinse discovered by the late Ron Thurman at the University of North Carolina, or UW solution, also known as ViaSpan) likely do not contain the same type of cardioprotective agent used in our studies that stimulated cyclic guanosine monophosphate (GMP) in heart tissues. Our EPR studies showed that the cardioprotection was probably due to nitric oxide released from nitrosoglutathione in the heart tissues. Thus, the opportunity to patent an MCW rinse was probably lost. John and I continued this work; however, we could not obtain continued funding for this project because of the lack of data from in vivo clinical and translational studies. John went on to do fascinating work on astronauts' risk for developing coronary heart disease following exposure to space radiation.

Again, I began searching for research projects that were timely, trending, important, and health-related, and that would have a likelihood of being funded. I attended a winter Gordon Conference meeting in Ventura, California. Gordon Conferences are relatively small; typically, the meetings are restricted to about 100–120 people. These meetings have a unique format.

Usually, there is a three-hour session from 9:00 a.m. to 12:00 p.m. with different invited speakers, and, unlike other conferences, there is generally plenty of time for discussion. The session chairs lead the discussion. That is where the action is; I love that part. If the audience has no questions, the chairs should drive the discussion in a way that encourages people to get involved. Again, the importance of all of this was ingrained in me by my graduate advisor. At the conference, I met Sam Parthasarathy who was a faculty in the Department of Medicine at the University of California, San Diego. Sam was an expert in lipid metabolism, and his research was related to lipid oxidation and how oxidatively modified lipid or low-density lipoprotein (LDL, i.e., bad cholesterol) is responsible for the process initiating the hardening of the arteries (atherosclerosis or arteriosclerosis). Sam co-authored many papers with Daniel Steinberg, a giant in the field of lipid metabolism and atherosclerosis. Michael Brown and Joseph Goldstein, recipients of the Nobel Prize for discovering statins (i.e., drugs that decrease cholesterol to optimum levels), invited Dan Steinberg to attend the Nobel Prize award ceremony and their accompanying lecture in Stockholm, Sweden, because they felt his scientific contributions were critical to some of their work. One time, when Sam invited me to give a seminar at the University of California, San Diego Medical School, I had the pleasure of dining with him and Dan. During dinner, we had grilled salmon, and I learned from Dan that, contrary to popular belief, both merlot and pinot noir pair perfectly well with salmon. Dan encouraged me to use EPR to understand the mechanism of oxidative modification of LDL. The evening was memorable.

I think it was Ian Smith from the National Research Council in Canada who told me that working on cholesterol was a good project, and there would always be NIH funding available because both Republicans and Democrats support cholesterol research as they are afraid of heart attacks. Sam offered to ship me freshly isolated LDL on ice every Thursday, so I would receive it the next day. He enclosed all the relevant information for oxidative modification experiments. I would work with that LDL over the weekend and ask for more on Monday; he would send another batch on Thursday. This went on for years. We were fortunate to get funded, and we did some good work that resulted in publications on the mechanism of lipid oxidation on LDL modification, and the effect of inhibiting lipid oxidation on macrophage degradation of oxidized LDL. Probably the most significant finding of our research was the discovery that nitric oxide acts as a much-superior chain-breaking antioxidant of LDL oxidation. Steve Goss, a graduate student in my lab, did most of this work, and Larry Keefer, from the Frederick National Laboratory in Maryland, collaborated on this project. Subsequently, the use of nitric oxide donors led to the discovery of novel nitrated lipids in Bruce Freeman's laboratory at the University of Alabama at Birmingham and later at the University of Pittsburgh.

Sam became a close friend, and over the years, he has provided an abundance of knowledge on many areas of my research. Recently, Sam passed away due to complications from COVID-19. A few days before he passed, he told me that I should be bold, try to surpass my ability, and do something I always wanted to do. I will miss Sam.

My interest in nitric oxide research was spurred by the feeling that my expertise in free radicals could contribute to advancing our knowledge of the chemical biology of nitric oxide. Nitric oxide is different from nitrous oxide (i.e., the laughing gas that dentists use). Nitric oxide is a common air pollutant found in automobile exhaust fumes. It is very unstable and reacts with oxygen to form nitrogen dioxide, which irritates eyes (among other things). Joseph Priestley, who discovered both oxygen and nitric oxide, liked smelling oxygen but not nitric oxide.

In 1993, I started the Nitric Oxide Journal Club at MCW. Its purpose was to discuss the chemical, biochemical, physiological, and methodological aspects of nitric oxide. It was a monumental success and continued for over ten years. The journal club met once a week, and the paper to be presented would be sent to the forty members ahead of time, so they came prepared. In those days, we did not have the technology to send the papers digitally, so our administrative assistant, Marian Krug, diligently sent paper copies to everyone. It did not matter how busy people were doing other things, most showed up for the journal club. It was gratifying to be told by Owen Griffith, chair of the Department of Biochemistry, that this weekly meeting was always on his calendar, and that he tried his best not to double-book this time slot. Owen discovered and developed the inhibitor of the nitric oxide synthase enzyme, L-NAME.

In 1998, I was invited to speak at the International Conference on Nitric Oxide in Graz, Austria. On the day of the meeting, I saw Joe Beckman and Jonathan Stamler, who I had met before, and Lou Ignarro in the hotel lobby. Lou was slated to give the plenary talk. As we walked from the hotel to the conference center, the conversation shifted to that year's Nobel Prize. Lou shared that he might have a shot at it if the Nobel Committee decided to give the prize for discovering nitric oxide as the molecule responsible for vascular relaxation induced by nitrovasodilators. But he wanted to be in the mix of two other scientists, Robert Furchgott and Ferid Murad, if the committee decided linking nitric oxide to endothelium-derived relaxing factor (EDRF) and/or linking cyclic GMP induced by nitric oxide-mediated signaling was more significant. So, Lou said he was going to focus on cyclic GMP and vasorelaxation. He explained that cigarette smoke, or cigarette smoke condensate, caused smooth muscle cell relaxation. Lou and his colleagues knew that cigarette smoke contains nitric oxide or nitric oxide-derived oxidation products, so they applied to a tobacco company for a grant investigating the mechanism of cigarette smoke-induced vasorelaxation. Lou said it was the easiest $300,000 grant he had ever gotten to do that type of research. This conversation happened during our walk to the conference center, months before the announcement of that year's Nobel Prizes. It is amazing how things worked out a few months later! The Nobel Prize in Physiology or Medicine was awarded to three scientists—Robert Furchgott, Lou Ignarro, and Ferid Murad— for the discovery of nitric oxide as a physiologically relevant signaling molecule produced in the cardiovascular system.

Pfizer's serendipitous discovery of Viagra is an interesting story. Sildenafil, the chemical name for Viagra, originally was developed to treat a heart condition, angina pectoris or chest pain, caused by a lack of blood flow due to constricted blood vessels supplying blood to the heart. The drug worked to perfection with respect to dilating the blood vessels. However, instead of dilating the vessels in the heart, it dilated the vessels in another part of the body, increasing blood flow to the penis. Serendipity in drug discovery happens. Viagra inhibits the enzyme phosphodiesterase that degrades cyclic GMP, resulting in the accumulation of this molecule. In the Phase I clinical trial, nurses noticed that male volunteers were on their stomachs because they were shy. In 1998, the US Food and Drug Administration approved Viagra for erectile dysfunction. Ten years later, the same drug was approved to treat pulmonary arterial hypertension in males and females. During this condition, blood flow to the lungs is restricted, and the drug with an active component, sildenafil, dilates the vessels in the lung. Ironically, in 2007, an Ig Nobel Prize—a satiric prize awarded annually to celebrate ten unusual or trivial achievements in scientific research—was awarded to three Argentinian scientists who discovered that hamsters quickly recover from jet lag when given Viagra. On a serious note, this may not be the end of the road for Viagra.

Emerging research from the Cleveland Clinic identified sildenafil as a candidate drug for vascular dementia. Increased cerebral blood flow and mitochondrial biogenesis induced by sildenafil were among the proposed mechanisms. These mechanisms are of extreme scientific interest, and clearly additional, randomized clinical trials are needed before establishing a link between the use of sildenafil and lowered risk of Alzheimer's disease and dementia.

The Nobel Prize was created by Alfred Nobel, who invented dynamite, an explosive made from nitroglycerine. During his later years, he suffered from angina pectoris, a lack of blood flow through the heart. The doctors prescribed nitroglycerin to treat this condition. Alfred Nobel said that it was the irony of fate that nitroglycerine, an explosive component he had discovered, was given to him as an oral medication. Now it is known that nitric oxide and cyclic GMP released from nitroglycerine are responsible for alleviating angina pectoris.

I met Robert Furchgott for the first time at a Photochemistry and Photobiology Meeting organized by the American Society for Photobiology in Chicago. I was the first speaker in the symposium on nitric oxide and was going to speak on the chemistry of nitric oxide. Before the symposium started, I was sitting in the front row, contemplating my talk. An elderly gentleman took the seat next to me and said that he was glad I was going to tell everyone about nitric oxide chemistry. He then introduced himself as Bob Furchgott; he was scheduled to be the second speaker. I then realized he was the same Robert Furchgott who'd won the Nobel Prize for discovering EDRF as nitric oxide. I told him that he should be the first speaker. He said, "No, I don't know anything about the chemistry of nitric oxide, and I hope that I learn more about nitric oxide chemistry from your talk." He was humility personified. I was more nervous giving that talk than any other time.

Robert Furchgott told the story about how, when doing experiments measuring the relaxation of isolated smooth muscle cells, he discovered the effect of light on smooth muscle relaxation. He noticed that the results of his experiments were erratic from day to day. He also observed a difference in relaxation, depending on whether the window shades were down or up. So, he deduced that visible light was responsible for generating a chemical species in smooth muscle cells that caused vascular relaxation.

When Robert Furchgott, Lou Iganarro, and Ferid Murad were asked, "What is EDRF?" Their answer was always, "I don't know." The chemical symbol for nitric oxide is NO, like the chemical symbol for oxygen is O2, and for water is H2O. They were all giving the correct, albeit cheeky, answer ("I don't NO") for EDRF, but no one realized that was the case. So, that mysterious thing formed inside the cells of our body and described as endothelial-derived relaxing factor is actually nitric oxide that is generated from the amino acid, L-arginine.

Some people in the vascular biology field thought that Salvador Moncada should have also shared the Nobel Prize. Salvador published a highly significant paper in *Nature* showing that the effects of EDRF were abrogated by compounds releasing superoxide, a reduced form of oxygen that is unstable and reactive. The enzyme, superoxide dismutase, originally discovered by Fridovich, restored the relaxation. This study suggested that superoxide reacts with EDRF. However, the actual identity of EDRF remained unknown. A few years later, Beckman, Freeman, Rafael Radi, and others at the University of Alabama at Birmingham, would go on to discover that superoxide is able to react with nitric oxide and form a very reactive species called peroxynitrite. Albert Szent-Györgyi (discoverer of vitamin C) once said, "Research is to see what everybody has seen and think what nobody has thought." Many researchers saw the relaxation of smooth muscles by acetylcholine, but it took three people to figure out the mechanism, which turned out to be the novel discovery of nitric oxide, as the most important signaling molecule in cells.

Salvador directed the Wellcome Research Laboratories in Kent, United Kingdom from 1986 to 1995. My friend Victor Darley-Usmar, currently at the University of Alabama at Birmingham, at the time was conducting research on nitric oxide, mitochondria, and oxidative modification of LDL. Lilian and I frequently visited Victor and his family. During one of my visits, Victor invited me to give a talk at Wellcome Research Laboratories. He took me to Salvador's office to introduce me but warned that Salvador likely would be too busy to spend any time with me, since he is rarely idle. Sure enough, Salvador was busy working on a manuscript but said he had five minutes. I started talking to him about my visit to San Diego, my collaboration with Steinberg's lab group, and Steinberg's idea of a cocktail antioxidant therapy for atherosclerosis, as well as a host of other topics associated with LDL oxidation and the modulatory role of nitric oxide. Victor and I spent about thirty minutes in Salvador's office; he was highly engaged and interested in redox mechanisms in cell signaling. Salvador talked about his discovery of how EDRF is abrogated by superoxide in endothelial cells. The conversation with Salvador was fascinating. After we left his office, Victor told me that was the most time he had ever spent in Salvador's office.

Seven years later, in 1998, in a key paper published in *PNAS*, we demonstrated that the enzyme, nitric oxide synthase, that is responsible for oxidizing L-arginine to nitric oxide, requires a molecule called tetrahydrobiopterin as a cofactor. In the absence of this cofactor or under conditions of decreased levels, this enzyme makes superoxide, a toxic species derived from oxygen. Jeannette Vásquez-Vivar, Pavel Martásek, Neil Hogg, Bettie Sue Masters, Hakim Karoui, Paul Tordo, Kirkwood Pritchard, and I co-authored the paper. This paper was communicated by Helmut Beinert, a member of the National Academy of Sciences, and the chair of the

EPR Center's advisory board. Jeannette used a technology developed by Jim Hyde and Wojciech Froncisz, and a probe developed by Paul Tordo in Marseille, France. Paul was director of the Material Science and Chemistry Department at Aix-Marseille Université. I served as an external reviewer on the dissertation committee of Hakim Karoui, one of Paul's graduate students. Later, Hakim joined my group as a postdoctoral fellow and was responsible for publishing several papers using the probe developed in Paul's laboratory. Paul and I became good friends. Another one of Paul's graduate students, Micael Hardy, joined my group later.

Micael has made ongoing contributions to the development of innovative mitochondria-targeted drugs that show promise as potential therapeutic drugs in cancer and Parkinson's disease.

Mike Murphy pioneered the use of a mitochondria-targeted antioxidant called MitoQ (a modified form of coenzyme Q) in mitigating the severity of inflammatory diseases. In 2016, Mike organized a meeting on mitochondrial metabolism on the outskirts Milton Keynes in Buckinghamshire, fifty miles northwest of London, United Kingdom.

Chicheley Hall, London, England. Photo credit: Balaraman Kalyanaraman.

I was invited to speak at the meeting, which was sponsored by the Royal Society. It took place in Chicheley Hall, an eighteenth-century country house that had been renovated and adapted to become a hotel and conference venue, set within eighty acres of beautifully maintained grounds. Each room at Chicheley Hall Hotel is named after a famous scientist from a different part of the world—Einstein, Bose, Ramanujan, Schrödinger, Bohr, etc.; Lilian and I stayed in the Rutherford Room.

This was a small meeting of fifty people, and during our meals in the beautiful dining room, we had the opportunity to meet nearly everyone in attendance. One day, Lilian and I were sitting at a table for breakfast. Salvador walked in and asked us if he could join us. I introduced Lilian to Sir Salvador Moncada, who had recently been knighted for his extraordinary contributions to science in many areas of vascular biology. In the 1990s, he was the second most cited scientist in the world. Lilian and Salvador started speaking in Spanish, each one sharing their stories about Cuba. I asked Salvador about the perks of receiving this highest honor from the Queen. He said he can go to any restaurant in the United Kingdom without making reservations. I am sure there are other perks he did not want to divulge.

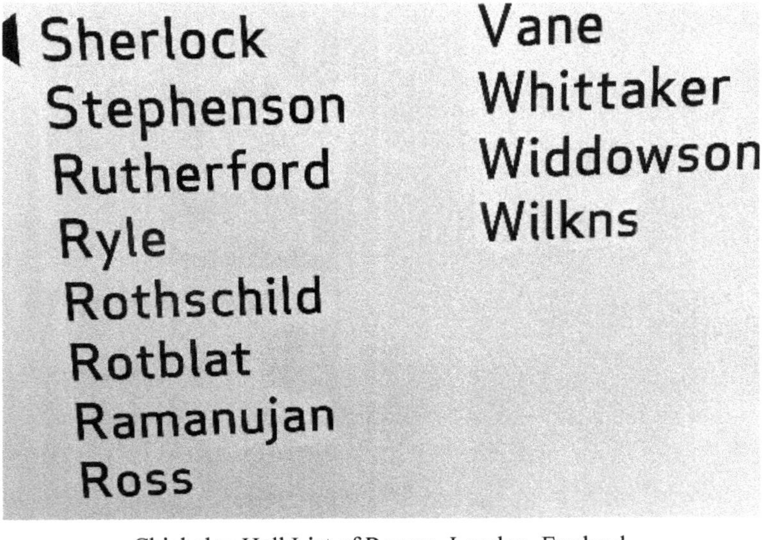

Chicheley Hall List of Rooms, London, England.

Salvador had an interest in promoting science in Latin America. I had not had a chance to visit Cuba, and I told Lilian that I was sure I could get over the visa hurdle through a scientific connection. I let Salvador know that I wanted to go to Cuba as a visiting scientist and asked whether he knew any neuroscience or cancer researchers there who could arrange that.

Salvador said, "How about both?" He told me that it would be taken care of and then went on to discuss his visits to Cuba. Apparently, Fidel Castro always wanted to meet with him; unfortunately, Castro was never on time. Once, Salvador had a dinner appointment with Castro around 6:00 p.m., and Castro's assistants told him that President Castro would be late but that he had arranged for a delightful dinner with Argentinian red wine. Finally, Salvador got to meet Castro in his office. Castro offered him a hand-crafted Cuban cigar and a 20-year-old single-malt whiskey and wanted to know everything about the latest and greatest in heart research, especially in the United States. Castro had asked his assistants not to disturb him, and their discussion of cardiovascular research, new drugs for treating cardiovascular diseases, and Alzheimer's and dementia research lasted until 5:00 the next morning.

Salvador's contacts from the Centro de Investigación y Desarrollo de Medicamentos (Drug Research and Development Center) in Havana reached out to me. They already had arranged for my talks and stay, and assured me they would also arrange for the visa. A few weeks later, I was notified that I should pick up my visa from the Embassy of Cuba in Washington, DC, a few days before my visit. Unfortunately, I had fallen ill a few weeks earlier and had to cancel the trip.

In 2000, I founded the MCW Free Radical Research Center. After Howard Jacob became the director of the Human and Molecular Genetics Center and moved to another lab, and David Harder took over as director of the Cardiovascular Research Center, he kindly offered the space to house the Free Radical Research

Center. It was a core facility for use by everyone at MCW. Rather than providing just the technical service, we provided the intellectual core facility. In some respects, it was a uniquely different approach at that time. David led an NIH-funded program project grant on free radicals in vascular signaling. David Harder was the principal investigator and David Gutterman, Peter Newman, and I had projects. We had a lot of fun putting the grant together—so much fun that before the grant was ready to be submitted, someone noticed there was no overall abstract. For some reason, it was not written.

Unfortunately, this was noticed after we had opened a bottle of champagne and had a few glasses. Most of us were in no shape to write the overall abstract, so Pete stepped in and saved the day. In any case, the proposal was funded. To this day, we think it was the abstract that made all the difference.

The MCW Free Radical Research Center became nationally and internationally recognized. I was fortunate to recruit postdoctoral fellows from Poland, Japan, Korea, China, India, France, the United States, Puerto Rico, and the United Kingdom, who shared a common interest in free radical research. We hear about free radicals in commercials for skin-care products and nutritional supplements. The Free Radical Research Center was one of the few dedicated research centers in the world in which the appropriate tools and technologies were developed to measure these free radicals in biological systems. Our motto at the Free Radical Research Center has been what the famous scientist William Thomas Kelvin preached years ago: "When you can measure what you are speaking about, and express it in numbers, you know something about it." Considering the discovery by Salvador of the EDRF reaction with superoxide, and the discovery by Beckman, Freeman, and Radi of the potential formation of a very potent oxidant species called peroxynitrite from the reaction between nitric oxide and superoxide, it was clear new research tools needed to be developed to detect and measure peroxynitrite in cells. I became aware of Chris Chang's research at the University of California, Berkeley; he was using a novel chemical probe called boronates to detect hydrogen peroxide. Adam Sikora from Poland spent a year in my laboratory and discovered that boronate-based compounds react rapidly with peroxynitrite, forming specific products that can be used as a diagnostic marker product.

This has opened the possibility of detecting intracellular formation of one of the most potent cellular oxidants.

I had been working with drugs like doxorubicin or Adriamycin (also known as "the red devil"), a widely used and highly effective chemotherapeutic drug, that can cause cardiotoxicity after treatment, sometimes ten to fifteen years later. These studies were all in cells, and I needed to branch out into animal models because the reviewers of my grants criticized me for not being relevant. In science, everyone is defined and branded initially by their graduate and postdoctoral education and expertise. That is where collaborations become necessary. At the time, Howard Jacob was working with chemically-induced breast cancer in a rat model, so I asked him if he was willing to collaborate with me. He said he would be happy to ask his colleagues, Donna McAllister and Sonia Sugg, to help me with my project and get the necessary in vivo data to address the reviewers' critiques. That marked the beginning of my cancer-related research. Thanks to Howard, that grant was funded, and it exemplifies how intramural researchers helping fellow researchers goes a long way in furthering the goals and mission of an institution. The best part of my collaboration with Howard is that I decided to pay it forward—to help others in need of my expertise without expecting anything in return.

Using the breast cancer rat model, we showed how doxorubicin-induced cardiotoxicity can be mitigated by mitochondria-targeted drugs like MitoQ. Cardiotoxicity is still a major problem with chemotherapy and needs to be addressed using preventative therapy. Someone once told me that patients who have been cured of breast cancer seek care not from oncologists, but from cardiologists, years after their successful chemotherapy.

As Russell Simmons said, the one way to achieve more in science is to "surround yourself with people who are smarter than you." Navdeep Chandel, a leading mitochondrial metabolism researcher at Northwestern University, called me about testing some of our mitochondria-targeted nitroxides on colon cancer cells. At exceedingly low levels, these compounds inhibited mitochondrial respiration selectively in cancer cells and inhibited their proliferation. In a paper published in *PNAS*, Nav, his colleagues, and my colleagues demonstrated that mitochondrial function is essential for cancer cell proliferation. Later, we showed that combining mitochondrial inhibitors with a glycolysis inhibitor synergistically and selectively caused cancer cell death. Continued collaboration and consultation with Nav played an essential role in my understanding of cancer versus normal cell metabolism.

Another person who shaped my understanding of cancer metabolism was Murali Krishna Cherukuri at NCI. Murali was using hyperpolarized MRI to monitor mitochondrial metabolism in cancer cells. As I was becoming interested in employing mitochondria-targeted drugs in cancer therapy, I realized the importance of using in vivo metabolic imaging in an animal model of cancer. Murali was primarily responsible for introducing me to the fascinating world of cancer metabolomics. He also participated in an NCI-funded multiple principal investigators grant that Mike Dwinell and I received to investigate the antitumor mechanism of a mitochondria-targeted drug called mito-metformin in pancreatic cancer.

Micael Hardy and Marcos Lopez, who were postdoctoral fellows in my lab, came up with the idea for mito-metformin. Metformin is one of the most prescribed drugs in the world for the treatment of diabetes. Micael and Marcos suggested it would be interesting to modify metformin such that it can more effectively target mitochondria. Micael successfully synthesized the mito-metformin, and our work with Mike Dwinell revealed that mito-metformin is a very potent drug in inhibiting pancreatic cancer progression in a mouse xenograft model of pancreatic cancer. This work is ongoing in our labs.

Ming You was hired as the director of the MCW Cancer Center in 2010. A long-standing objective of the MCW Cancer Center has been to achieve the NCI-designated Comprehensive Cancer Center status. There are approximately 155 medical schools in the United States, and about half of them have NCI-Designated Cancer Centers. Wisconsin is home to the Carbone Comprehensive Cancer Center at the University of Wisconsin–Madison. If Froedtert & the MCW Clinical Cancer Center attain the prestigious NCI designation, they can better serve the most populous counties in southeastern Wisconsin, as well as address disparities in cancer incidence and outcomes for underrepresented populations. Frank Wilson, Larry Hopwood, Robert Truitt, Sidney Grossberg, Bruce Campbell, and Chris Chitambar contributed substantially to the evolution of the MCW Cancer Center. We needed a dedicated person to provide strategic leadership and direction.

Ming knew what needed to be done. He systematically put in place infrastructure that did not exist at MCW prior to his recruitment. Ming recognized that one of the most critical requirements for a successful NCI designation is to establish core facilities that are unique and do not duplicate the efforts of the core facilities at other cancer centers in the United States. He chose cancer biology as one of the thematic areas. Because I was one of the few investigators who had NCI-funded grants at that time, he asked me to lead the Cancer Biology Program.

Although I worked with chemotherapeutic drugs, I did not consider myself as a bona fide cancer researcher. I felt the program would benefit from having input from someone who was actively investigating cell signaling, so I asked Carol Williams to serve as the co-director of the program, and she graciously accepted. Carol hit the ground running and was largely responsible for building the Cancer Biology Program at the MCW Cancer Center. For my part, I started the Redox and Bioenergetics Shared Resource. This core facility, presently directed by Jacek Zielonka who worked in my lab for several years, helps MCW cancer investigators and other researchers obtain state-of-the-art analyses of mitochondrial oxidative metabolism, reactive oxygen species formation, and detoxification of oxidants by mitochondrial antioxidant enzymes in cells and tissues, and then relate these parameters to redox signaling and cell proliferation.

The expertise to provide detailed information on redox mechanisms in cancer cells is unique and is crucial to our understanding of mitochondrial metabolism in cancer therapy, cancer diversity, and immuno-oncology. After Ming You's departure from the Cancer Center, Gustavo Leone succeeded him as the MCW Cancer Center director. Gustavo inherited a well-established cancer center with a strong infrastructure to build upon. I decided to step down as co-director of the Cancer Biology Program, which is in good hands. Now, there is also much more financial commitment from MCW's administration. In fact, MCW is building a 150,000-square-foot, state-of-the-art facility dedicated to cancer research; it is expected to be completed by late 2024.

Overall, these transitions have been win-win for everyone, and I am still collaborating with Ming, who is now director of the Center for Cancer Prevention at Houston Methodist Research Institute. Our ultimate goal is to get our patented mitochondria-targeted drugs to cancer patients.

Our research involving mitochondria-targeted drug therapy for cancer originated from our ongoing experiments in Parkinson's disease research. Our rationale was that cancer cells need an abundant supply of nutrients to provide energy to support the rapidly proliferating cells.

Inhibition of mitochondrial respiration and adenosine triphosphate synthesis would, therefore, have a more potent antiproliferative effect in cancer cells than in normal cells. This turned out to be an interesting approach. Several novel drugs were synthesized in collaboration with Joy Joseph, a Biophysics faculty member, and Micael. We are now repurposing these drugs from Parkinson's disease research to cancer therapy.

In the mid-1980s, I became interested in neurodegeneration research, Parkinson's disease in particular. This coincided with the finding that the chemical MPTP (which initially was discovered as a contaminant of an illicit narcotic) induced Parkinson-like symptoms in experimental animals. Emerging research at that time linked a toxic metabolite of MPTP to increased free radical formation in brain mitochondria, disruption of mitochondrial respiration, and neuronal cell death. Because of the structural similarity between the MPTP metabolite and paraquat, a free radical-generating herbicide linked to environmental Parkinsonism, there was increased interest in the basic free radical chemistry of MPTP. My goal was to understand the mechanistic steps involved in the transformation of MPTP to the ultimate toxic metabolite and oxygen-derived radicals in brain mitochondria. These studies led to the publication of three papers. However, during that time, I was unsuccessful in obtaining NIH funds to continue these studies.

My research direction then turned to other areas related to nitric oxide and its role in vasodilatory mechanisms, myocardial ischemia, and reperfusion injury. In the late 1990s, researchers proposed a role for nitric oxide in MPTP-mediated neuronal cell death. My interest in Parkinson's research was rekindled, and in collaboration with Cecilia "Cece" Hillard (professor of pharmacology & toxicology and director of the MCW Neuroscience

Research Center), we prepared a research proposal that linked MPTP to increased free radical formation in the brain through altered metabolism of nitric oxide. The proposal was funded by the National Institute of Neurological Disorders and Stroke in 1999 and was subsequently renewed in 2004 for another four years. During this period, we made important discoveries about the neuroprotective role of an endogenous pterin biochemical (sepiapterin), an important cofactor in the synthesis of neuronal nitric oxide, and its connection to iron-dependent mitochondrial oxidative damage in neuronal cells exposed to the MPTP metabolite. Shasi Kalivendi, who was a postdoctoral fellow in my group and is presently senior principal scientist at the Centre for Chemical Biology at the Indian Institute of Chemical Technology, contributed largely to this project. These results led us to propose that mitochondria-targeted antioxidants might afford increased neuroprotection against MPTP toxicity. Together with Anumantha Kanthasamy, who led the team from Iowa State University, we submitted the first multiple principal investigator proposal that was funded by the National Institute of Neurological Disorders and Stroke.

For my work on the role of oxidative stress on the mitochondria in Parkinson's disease, and how antioxidants targeted to mitochondria might interrupt the development of Parkinson's symptoms in cellular and animal models, in 2009, I was honored and humbled to be the first to receive the title Harry R. and Angeline E. Quadracci Professor in Parkinson's Research at MCW. Brothers Harry, Len, and Tom Quadracci created the endowment in honor of their mother and father. I am grateful to MCW and to the Quadracci family for allowing me to think freely and try new, bold research ideas that could be useful in Parkinson's disease treatment and in enhancing the quality of life of patients with Parkinson's disease.

We discovered one of our mitochondria-targeted drugs (a modification of a naturally occurring chemical, apocynin) greatly improved neuronal function and decreased neuroinflammation in a Parkinson's mouse model. Parkinson's disease is a chronic neurodegenerative disease affecting a part of the brain, the substantia nigra. Dopamine, an important neurotransmitter, is slowly depleted over the years and leads to decreased motor function and other symptomatic events. If we live for more than 100 years, nearly everyone will have some Parkinson's-like syndrome. However, there are many factors, such as exposure to chemicals and environmental pesticides, that can hasten the process of neurodegeneration.

Thus, it is difficult to pinpoint a single animal model of Parkinson's disease that can accurately mimic the disease progression. This is also a reason for the lack of therapeutic success in the treatment of Parkinson's disease.

Diminished ability to smell and detect odors (a condition known as hyposmia) is one of the early signs of Parkinson's disease onset. This condition leads to a loss of interest in food, causing weight loss and muscle weakness, affecting quality of life. In lab experiments, we showed that one of the drugs developed improves the olfactory function responsible for smell. Alison Gifford, the research technologist who was working on this project with one of my postdoctoral fellows, Brian Dranka, was responsible for this discovery. The sense of smell was tested in mice. Each cage contained both a buried chow pellet and a fruit-scented cereal treat. These mice were not conditioned for the "buried treat smell test." The time required to locate either a chow pellet or a fruit-scented cereal was determined for control mice and transgenic mice with Parkinson's-like symptoms, and our mitochondria-targeted drug treated transgenic mice with Parkinson's-like symptoms. The experiment was videotaped. Control mice located the chow pellet or fruit-scented cereal treat quickly, within seconds. However, mice with the Parkinson's-like symptoms took nearly a couple of minutes to locate the fruit-scented cereal treat. Treatment with the mitochondria-targeted drug (mito-apocynin) in mice with Parkinson's-like symptoms dramatically decreased the time (a few seconds) to locate the fruit-scented cereal treat. These findings suggest that the olfactory function in the Parkinson's disease mouse model was restored upon treatment with the mitochondria-targeted drug. I hope that with appropriate clinical trials, we may be able to use mitochondria-targeted drugs to restore the sense of smell in individuals in the early stages of Parkinson's disease.

We are currently exploring ways to enhance the therapeutic efficacy of levodopa, also called L-dopa. Recent research suggests L-dopa is metabolized to dopamine in the gut of individuals with Parkinson's disease. This greatly decreases the amount of L-dopa that reaches the brain and its conversion to dopamine in the brain, where it acts as an important neurotransmitter.

So, if we can inhibit the bacterial metabolism of L-dopa in the gut (without causing any side effects in the gut microbiome), more L-dopa will reach the brain, resulting in more dopamine formation in the brain. This work is being performed in conjunction with Cece and Jimmy Feix. Gang Cheng, who worked with me as a postdoctoral fellow and is now assistant professor of Biophysics, is also involved with this project.

In 2010, I received the honorary title of ad honorem professor of medicine at the Universidad de la República, the oldest and largest public university in Uruguay. Our family trip to Montevideo, the capital of Uruguay, was memorable. We flew there from Miami. Rafael Radi, professor, and chair of the Departamento de Bioquímica, invited me to give a talk in his department for this occasion. Rafael and Silvina Bartesaghi were excellent hosts, and we had a great time. One of the highlights of the trip was a three-hour ferryboat trip from Montevideo to Buenos Aires, the capital of Argentina. Seeing the skyline of Buenos Aires as we approached the city was spectacular. If you could get to the front of the upper deck of the ferry, you could feel the *buenos aires* (good breezes). My family and I stayed at the Hilton Hotel in the western part of the city. Rafael had previously arranged with Alberto Boveris at the University of Argentina to host us. I remember meeting Boveris at a Society for Free Radical Research International meeting and knew of his seminal contributions to mitochondrial metabolism. Boveris and Britton Chance pioneered the concept that reactive oxygen species are generated at a very low level (0.1%) during mitochondrial respiration, and their level can be increased from dysfunctional mitochondria. The concept of mitochondrial oxidative stress originated from the works of Boveris, Helmut Sies, Enrique Cadenas, Julio Turrens, and Chance. The credit for coining the phrase "oxidative stress" goes to Sies. Boveris took us to a nice restaurant serving fine Argentinian food and malbec wine from the Mendoza region.

I was involved in the early days of the creation of the Center for Research on Redox Processes in Biomedicine (also the Redoxoma Center) in São Paulo, Brazil. This center is supported by a FAPESP program of the Brazilian Government. Ohara Augusto, a member of the Brazilian Academy of Sciences and an accomplished researcher in free radical chemistry and biochemistry, is the director of the center. I served on the International Advisory Board for the Redoxoma Center along with Rafael and Gary Fiskum from the University of Maryland. The Redoxoma Center is a dynamic network consisting of outstanding of scientists in basic science, applied science, and clinical research. Jeannette Vásquez-Vivar, supported by this program under the guidance of Ohara, came to MCW as a postdoctoral fellow and is now a professor of biophysics. I met Jeannette, who was then a postdoctoral fellow at the University of São Paulo, at one of the Society for Free Radical Research conferences in Australia, where she presented her work on the EPR detection of free radicals using a specialized technique called spin trapping. Impressed by the quality of her research, I asked her if she wanted to work as a postdoctoral fellow in Milwaukee. She asked, "*Dónde está Milwaukee*?" I told her it is near Chicago, Illinois, and she immediately knew the location. A few months later, Jeannette joined MCW and started working with Kirkwood Pritchard and me. Her work resulted in our *PNAS* paper that became a citation classic.

I will never forget my trip to Hanover, New Hampshire, September 6–10, 2001, to attend an EPR meeting on in vivo spectroscopy and imaging, organized by Hal Swartz, who was a professor of radiology at Dartmouth Medical School. After the meeting, I took the bus to the Boston Logan Airport to catch the Midwest Express flight to Milwaukee. When I checked in at the airport, the airline ticket agent told me the flight was delayed due to bad weather conditions in the Midwest and the plane had not yet left Milwaukee. That meant a delay of more than five hours. I was worried the flight would be canceled if weather conditions did not improve and asked to be booked on the nine o'clock flight the next day. The friendly agent told me she was based in Milwaukee and that she, too, was looking forward to getting home that night. She recommended I have a Sam Adams beer and burger at the Cheers Restaurant and said time would fly and that I would get home that night. I asked whether they would serve warm chocolate chip cookies on the flight, the trademark of Midwest Express, and she replied, "You betcha" (a classic midwestern phrase for "absolutely"). Feeling reassured, I took a seat at the Cheers Restaurant bar. I ordered a burger, fries, and a pint of Sam Adams, and started chitchatting with a bunch of guys from a rock group headed to Chicago for a gig. Their flight also was delayed. After sticking around for an hour, they decided to stay the night in Boston and take the show on the road the next day. I don't know when they got out of Boston. After some time, I learned the plane from Milwaukee had finally arrived. We immediately started boarding and left Boston around 11:00 p.m., arriving in Milwaukee after 1:00 a.m.

Later that morning, I woke up late, turned on the TV, and found out the World Trade Center had been hit. Two planes that had taken off from the Boston Logan Airport were hijacked and flown into the Twin Towers in New York. Every airport was closed, and the world as we knew it was changed. I kept that boarding pass as a bookmark for several years, as a reminder of those who lost their lives on 9/11.

Fast forward to a recent annual one-on-one conversation with MCW President John Raymond; I told him that, in my forty or so years of working at MCW, there was not a single day that I wasn't excited to come to work. This is because I work with amazing people. Some days (when the weather is nice), it takes me thirty minutes to get from the parking lot to my office because I meet colleagues and collaborators along the way, and we catch up on research and a host of other things. I agree with Steve Jobs' quote: "The only way to do great work is to love what you do." I didn't realize my work was great until August 2020, when I received MCW's Distinguished Service Award, which is the institution's highest honor. I thank William Campbell, former chair of the Department of Pharmacology and Toxicology, for nominating me for the award and my many other colleagues for writing letters of support.

Considering all the individuals who helped me along my career path, and provided mentorship, I made it a priority to help others in the same way. I have found this to be an important factor in achieving professional success and satisfaction. Typically, leaders are pressed for time and faced with deadlines and commitments; however, whenever feasible, I believe leaders should go the extra mile to serve their institution and mentor young scientists, junior faculty, and colleagues. In the biomedical sciences, this comes in several forms: Serving on institutional committees, reviewing research grant proposals, participating in study section reviews of pilot grant proposals, helping to read and critique proposals and manuscripts from colleagues and junior faculty, training underrepresented minority students in research, and participating in other mentoring activities related to professional growth. I have written hundreds of letters of support and have had countless discussions with junior faculty at MCW. Although these activities are time-consuming, I find them infinitely rewarding and am pleased when these individuals succeed in their own endeavors and contributions.

Chapter 9
THE YEAR 2020: A VIRAL TRANSFORMATION

"No one will ever be truly safe until everyone is safe."
—Amina Mohammed

Amina Mohammed, deputy secretary-general of the United Nations and chair of the United Nations Sustainable Development Group, posted the above-quoted text on Twitter. This quote has been used repeatedly to remind people across the globe that SARS-CoV-2 affects everyone and is not limited to any one nation or region; it reinforces the idea that, if anyone—especially vulnerable populations in low-income countries—is excluded from access to the vaccine, the transmission of this virus or its variants will never be stopped. The World Health Organization established the COVAX (COVID-19 Vaccines Global Access) scheme, and their vision is captured in their name. But their vision did not go as planned. By the time people in low-income countries started receiving vaccines, the variants had begun to escalate in high-income countries, who then kept more vaccines for their own use; this vicious cycle continues. With respect to combating pandemics, the oft-quoted, nationalistic slogan, "charity begins at home," goes out the window. Thinking and acting globally is the only way to return to normal.

The joke among ophthalmologists was that 2020 was going to be a *perfect* year. But clearly that wasn't the case. Life as we knew it came to a screeching halt in March 2020 as the global COVID-19 pandemic spread rapidly. Nearly half the world's population was under some type of lockdown; in Wisconsin, we had a Safe at Home Order. I—like much of the rest of the world—sat at home every day watching the news reports that people infected with SARS-CoV-2 were admitted into intensive care units, placed on ventilators, and died of respiratory failure following massive lung damage due to COVID-19. Face coverings were offered as a solution to prevent the spread of the virus, just as they were used nearly 100 years ago to prevent the spread of the 1918 influenza epidemic. Disinfecting all surfaces, frequent hand washing, and social distancing were suggested as additional preventive measures.

Virologists, immunologists, and chemists worked feverishly behind the scenes to produce a vaccine for the virus. For the first time, scientists from across the globe shared information that advanced our understanding of the virus, its mechanism of action, and potential antidotes, literally minute by minute. I wanted to be involved and contribute my two cents to this cause. Initially, I wrote a light-hearted article on face coverings and social distancing (Kalyanaraman 2020a). After a few months of research and reading the literature, I realized an immune mechanism of action that was common in both cancer and COVID-19 was also the plausible reasoning for the disproportionate COVID-19-related deaths among Black/African Americans and Hispanics/Latinx (Kalyanaraman 2021b). I also realized that, even if vaccines became available, overcoming racial disparities in vaccination posed a major barrier. This prompted me to think about racial disparities in clinical trials. I decided to write a piece discussing racial disparities in medicine, as a step toward rebuilding trust (Kalyanaraman 2020b). Also, I was drawn to early discoveries on synthetic chemistry of messenger RNA molecules by Katalin Karikó, PhD, the Hungarian scientist who was partly responsible for developing the COVID-19 vaccine. During lockdown, the reoccurring theme was to reimagine everything we did and adapt to a new way of life during the pandemic. So, I wrote an article that considers how we can reimagine many aspects of our lives as well as our research (and includes the inspiring story of a COVID-19 researcher to whom we all owe a debt of gratitude), our relationships, and our health (Kalyanaraman 2021a). The following sections contain the articles (with a few minor adaptations) I published in the *Transformational Times*, a newsletter by the MCW Kern Institute for the Transformation of Medical Education (Kalyanaraman 2020a, b, 2021a), as well as an excerpt from the article "Reactive oxygen species, proinflammatory and immunosuppressive mediators induced in COVID-19: overlapping biology with cancer" that I published in *RSC Chemical Biology* (Kalyanaraman 2021b).

EVERY VIRUS NEEDS A HOST AND THE ANSWER LIES WITHIN EACH OF US

I don't know about you, but the terms "social distancing," "self-quarantining," "asymptomatic," and "flattening the curve" were all new to me! It took me a while to figure out that social distancing is not the same as anti-social, and that self-quarantining is not a punishment.

Apparently, social distancing existed in medieval times and was used to fight the bubonic plague. Here is some historical "viral" news that may interest you.

SIR ISAAC NEWTON

Sir Isaac Newton (1643–1727), a transformative scholar, inventor, and writer, made all his discoveries in the fields of calculus, astronomy, optics, and gravitation while in isolation. In case you are new to social distancing history, here is my take.

Twenty-three-year-old Newton was studying at the University of Cambridge in England in 1665, when London was hit with the Great Plague. The university temporarily closed, and Newton went to his family home in the countryside. Even then, the rate of infection was recognized to be much higher in densely populated cities than in the rural areas. He used his time off wisely and started to think boldly in isolation. No emails from or videoconferencing with professors! No social media! Newton spent a lot of time musing under an apple tree in the backyard, and legend has it that one afternoon he was bonked on the head by a falling apple. Rather than being miffed about it, he wondered why the apple fell straight rather than swerving, going up, or going sideways! Well, there you have it—the discovery of gravitational force. Newton also postulated the three laws of motion:

Every body remains in a state of rest or uniform motion unless acted upon by a net external force.

How true! I saw it in a health club. Good motivational messaging! Now that I stopped going to the health club because of COVID, I try to social distance with the refrigerator.

The amount of acceleration of a body is proportional to the acting force and inversely proportional to the mass of the body; f = ma.

*I don't know why your car is so f@#*king damaged when you hit a deer at 70 mph.*

For every action, there is an equal but opposite reaction.

Hmm, does this remind you of what is going on in politics here and around the world?

Having worked out his theories on gravitation, calculus, and laws of motion, Newton returned to Cambridge after the plague subsided. He went from student to full professor in two years. By the way, the two years Newton spent in isolation and discovering new theories of nature are known as *annus mirabilis* or "remarkable years." Who knows? Some of our graduate students may realize 2020 was their *annus mirabilis!*

SIR WILLIAM SHAKESPEARE

Many artists completed their classic works during isolation from a pandemic. Sir William Shakespeare (1564–1616) was one of them. Shakespeare was an actor, shareholder, and playwright. After an outbreak of bubonic plague, London's theatres shut down and Shakespeare was out of a job! He decided to use his free time to write plays, including masterpieces like *King Lear* and *Macbeth*. However, Shakespeare's most plague-inspired play was *Romeo and Juliet*, in which the plague and quarantine play a prominent role in the plot. Here are some *Romeo and Juliet* highlights and my thoughts on what Shakespeare can teach us all amid COVID-19. Juliet and Romeo, from two feuding families in Verona, Italy, were in love but their families did not approve of their relationship. So, they secretly arranged to elope. In the meantime, Juliet's family decided she would marry someone else. Juliet's mentor had a counterplan to put her to sleep with a clever drug that would make her appear dead. A letter describing this plan was arranged to be delivered to Romeo. *Spoiler alert*: Romeo did not get the message because the messenger was quarantined and could not leave Verona due to the plague. You know the rest of the story.

THE TUSKEGEE STUDY: OVERCOMING RACIAL DISPARITIES IN VACCINATIONS AND REBUILDING THE TRUST OF BLACK AMERICANS

"Injustice anywhere is a threat to justice everywhere.
We are caught in an inescapable network of mutuality,
tied in a single garment of destiny.
Whatever affects one directly,
affects all indirectly."
—Dr. Martin Luther King, Jr.

Racial disparity in vaccination is a sensitive topic. I am not an expert in this area; however, I want to address this issue because it is timely, and a matter of life and death with COVID-19.

Black Americans are at increased risk of contracting SARS-CoV-2, nearly five times more likely to be hospitalized from COVID-19, and twice as likely to die from it as compared with White Americans. In the past, safe and effective vaccines saved millions of lives against pandemic viruses, yet the perception on vaccines and vaccinations remains varied among different groups struggling to decide whether to get vaccinated. Many people have lingering doubts about vaccine safety and even the motives behind vaccination. People have either forgotten about the Tuskegee Study or never heard of it. Reopening old wounds is not my current objective, but I believe that knowing about and contemplating events of injustice in history make all of us better and will ensure that such acts are never repeated. Accurate information empowers people to make informed decisions. Encouraging Black American participation in vaccination, especially during the COVID-19 pandemic, should be a top priority.

TUSKEGEE SYPHILIS STUDY

Tuskegee is in Macon County, Alabama, about 120 miles southeast of Birmingham. I was a graduate student in chemistry from 1974 to 1978 at the University of Alabama in Tuscaloosa, which is about 140 miles west of Tuskegee. The news about the Tuskegee Study broke in 1972. Having newly arrived from India in the midst of it all, I was clueless; I did not even know where Tuskegee was, let alone anything about the Tuskegee Study.

I found out about Tuskegee after I became a fan of Lionel Richie of *The Commodores*. Richie was born in Tuskegee, and completed his undergraduate degree in economics at the Tuskegee Institute. The song "Easy (Like Sunday Morning)" is still one of my favorites, especially on Sundays. The real implications of the Tuskegee Study dawned on me only a few weeks ago, when I was watching a Sunday morning program discussing COVID-19 vaccinations, and why Black Americans are skeptical, suspicious, and even fearful of vaccines. The reason for their mistrust in vaccines? *Well, Tuskegee always looms large in their minds.*

What exactly was the Tuskegee Study? Nearly ninety years ago, the US Public Health Service began a clinical study in Tuskegee in which they enrolled 600 Black men with and without syphilis. Many were enticed to participate with incentives such as free medical exams and meals, and even burial insurance. There was no informed consent. These men were not aware that they were participating in a study about syphilis; rather, they were told they would be treated for "bad blood," the local term for various ailments ranging from fatigue and anemia to syphilis. When the study began in 1932, there was no known treatment for syphilis. Thirteen years later, penicillin became the standard treatment for syphilis, yet it was withheld from the subjects who were infected. When asked why the study was not halted after determining that penicillin cured syphilis, the answer was: *Never again would they find such cohort of "untreated" syphilis patients for medical information on organ damage*.

As a result, many untreated men died of syphilis, and others suffered severe syphilis-related cardiovascular and neurological complications that persisted for years.

The legacy of the exploitive and unethical Tuskegee Study contributed to racial disparities in health-care utilization and has had a long-lasting negative impact on the willingness of Black Americans to participate in clinical trials or vaccinations.

INCREASING THE PARTICIPATION OF BLACK AMERICANS IN CLINICAL TRIALS AND VACCINATIONS

How can health-care professionals dispel suspicions about clinical trials and vaccines, and regain the trust of Black Americans in vaccination? Finding a way for Black Americans to get past medical mistrust involves accurate and credible messaging as to why participation is important.

Diseases have disparate impacts on people depending on gender, race, ethnicity, age, and related factors, and drugs often exert different effects in different people. This is a whole new area of science known as pharmacogenetics—the science that reveals how genetic factors affect reactions to drugs and vaccinations. Thus, research protocols for clinical trials should include women, Black/African Americans, Hispanics/Latinx, and other racial and ethnic minorities in addition to White men. To ensure no group experiences untoward side effects in response to drug treatment, it is also necessary to increase the number of participants in each group.

Motivation to participate in clinical trials is often personal and is triggered by different events in people's lives. This is where science can help. Sharing clinical success stories of scientific discoveries revolutionizing treatment of sickle cell disease, which predominantly affects people of African descent, is definitely encouraging! Most people know what DNA is and why it is important in life. That editing and correcting one error in the DNA of sickle cell patients could become a treatment or even a cure for this disease is likely to resonate better. This discovery was made possible because of participation in clinical trials.

As for vaccines, (1) communicate the best available, credible science on vaccine safety and the risks versus benefits of vaccination; (2) explain how the vaccine was developed and managed with independent oversight and advisory groups; and (3) empower by providing available data from pharmaceutical companies on their trial protocols (e.g., how many Black volunteers participated in Phases I, II, and III of the clinical trials). Big pharmaceutical companies (e.g., AstraZeneca, Moderna, Johnson & Johnson, Pfizer) received our tax dollars to develop COVID-19 vaccines, and numerous trials are currently ongoing.

It is essential to effectively convey the clinical objectives of each trial phase. For example: A Phase I trial consists of a small number of volunteers and will determine the safety and dosing of the vaccine and whether the immune system (through the generation of antibodies) is activated in people receiving the vaccine. In Phase I, vaccines are given to healthy people, so the tolerated side effects are minimal. In Phase II, the objectives are similar, but the goal is to assess whether the drug works, and more volunteers are enrolled. In Phase III, a larger number of volunteers is enrolled. By Phase III, the safety of the vaccine will already have been established for most people, but information continues to be gathered on a vaccine's side effects and how well it works. The incidence of infections in the treatment group compared with the placebo group determines the effectiveness of the vaccine.

All phases of clinical studies have clear, prespecified guidelines on what adverse side effects are acceptable and what side effects would halt the clinical trial. Vaccine trials are typically placebo-controlled and double-blind. Placebo-controlled means that half of the volunteers receive placebo (e.g., salt water) and the other half receive the vaccine. Double-blind means no one involved in the study (not the volunteer, health professionals, or sponsors) knows which treatment (i.e., placebo or vaccine) is given. The clinical trial is closely watched by an independent data safety monitoring board whose main function is to monitor the safety and efficacy of a trial, and who has the authority to halt a trial if the side effects are severe.

Ultimately, the objective of providing this type of information from reliable, trusted sources is to empower people with facts about clinical trials and vaccines so they can make informed decisions.

FIGHTING FEAR WITH FACTS ON VACCINES AND VACCINE DISTRIBUTION

Fears about vaccines can be dispelled by facts. Most vaccines fail in Phase III, but the likelihood of success of a COVID-19 vaccine is greater because the vaccines against COVID-19 are built on related coronaviruses (MERS and SARS). Historical data show that the efficacy of vaccines against respiratory viruses (transmitted by breathing and talking) is low. However, even if the COVID-19 vaccine is 60% effective (i.e., if the vaccine prevents COVID-19 in six out of ten recipients), it is considered very good. The FDA has set a bar of at least 50% efficacy (i.e., the vaccine prevents COVID-19 in five out of ten recipients) for the COVID-19 vaccine.

Who will receive the vaccines first? No one should feel like a guinea pig. Independent advisory panels and the Centers for Disease Control and Prevention make determinations based on the social vulnerability index. The first recipients may include frontline workers, healthcare personnel, the elderly, and people with underlying medical conditions (e.g., diabetes, hypertension). Black Americans are at a far higher risk of contracting the COVID-19 and dying from it.

To lessen this disparity and empower people to make informed decisions, healthcare professionals must share accurate information from trusted sources.

POPULATIONS THAT HAVE BEEN HISTORICALLY MARGINALIZED IN BIOMEDICAL RESEARCH

Black and Hispanic cancer patients have increased cancer mortality. Many factors (such as socioeconomic differences and insufficient access to health care) contribute to racial disparity. Emerging research implicates biological disparity in cancer outcomes. Studies show distinct differences in the tumor immune microenvironment in Black cancer patients, implicating an increased role for oxidative phosphorylation in racial disparity. Mitochondria-targeted drugs are, therefore, developed to overcome the biological disparity in cancer mortality.

The tumor immune microenvironment in Black cancer patients consists of more pro-tumorigenic factors and mitochondrial dysfunction than in White cancer patients. Thus, developing a highly potent, less toxic, and tumor/tumor immune microenvironment-selective next generation of mitochondrial oxidative phosphorylation inhibitors is timely and critical in overcoming racial and ethnic disparities in cancer treatment. Poor accrual of Black and Hispanic cancer patients in clinical trials has hindered our understanding of the biological basis of racial disparity. Clinical trials should include Black and Hispanic cancer patients and new and evolving combinatorial cancer treatments.

REIMAGINE: IT'S EASY IF YOU *TRY*

"Anything you do I can do better, but only if you do it first. That's because I have no imagination, only a re-imagination."
—Andrew Keith Walker

Right now, I bet you are telling someone, or have been asked, to reimagine some aspect of your work or life. Or perhaps you are reading about or watching an advertisement focused on reimagining. But what does reimagine mean? According to Merriam-Webster, the first use of the word was in 1825, and it is now among the top 1% of words that are looked up. I don't know about you, but the word "imagine" makes me happy; hearing it frees up space in my brain. Conversely, the word "reimagine" makes me feel tense and anxious; it sounds task oriented and somewhat contrived! Well, the more I've pondered the word "reimagine," the more I've realized I do not have to feel this way!

While trying to understand "reimagine," I came across this anecdote about imagination from the book *The Element: How Finding Your Passion Changes Everything* by Ken Robinson, PhD:

> An elementary school teacher was giving a drawing class to a group of six-year-old children. At the back of the classroom sat a little girl who normally didn't pay much attention in school. In the drawing class she did. For more than twenty minutes, the girl sat with her arms curled around her paper, totally absorbed in what she was doing. The teacher found this fascinating. Eventually, she asked the girl what she was drawing. Without looking up, the girl said, "I'm drawing a picture of God." Surprised, the teacher said, "But nobody knows what God looks like." The girl said, "They will in a minute."

The girl was making an image of something she could not feel with her senses but could feel in her heart!

Try to reimagine "Imagine" written by John Lennon and inspired by Yoko Ono:

Imagine there's no heaven
It's easy if you try
No hell below us
Above us, only sky
Imagine all the people
Living for today

Hmm, the song is not the same when reimagined, right? Clearly, reimagination requires imagination with a lot of passion!

In business, people "think outside the box" and reimagine everything from A to Z! (Do you have a novel idea? Sorry! Amazon already claimed it.) I considered synonyms for reimagine: reconceptualize, re-envision, reinvent, rethink, refine, re-create, re-evaluate, or reinterpret imaginatively. It seems that "reimagine" is a word meant to inspire us; it captures the essence of what we need to do together or in collaboration that builds upon our strength.

In the following sections, I've given my thoughts on reimagining a few aspects of research and life that are personal to me, but I know there are plenty more that you can reimagine. Some of these also could be applicable to other areas, such as workplaces, social systems, communication, teaching, childcare, sports, and recreation.

REIMAGINING IDEAS IN RESEARCH

How does one reimagine research ideas? Here are some ways to get started:

To find one good idea, you ought to begin with several ideas. It's important, though, to work on only one idea at a time.

Become obsessed with your idea. Believe in yourself, but be prepared to modify your idea.

Always be ready to talk about your research ideas passionately at different levels depending upon your audience.

Don't be afraid to talk to your colleagues about the grant that was not scored or did not score well enough to be funded, even if they are not in your field!

Rejection happens to everyone, no matter your reputation in your field. Even Nobel Laureates experience it. Ideas, new and old, are rejected all the time. What matters is how you respond to criticism and reshape your ideas!

Even though you may have the most cutting-edge idea, your proposal may lack widespread approval in the study section and require tweaking. Sometimes you have not exactly read between the lines in the summary statement, and you keep resubmitting the same idea while expecting different results. This is when you really need to get out of your comfort zone and reimagine—consider a chemist/biochemist collaborating with an immunologist, a vaccine researcher (perhaps, an extreme example)!

A GREAT EXAMPLE OF REIMAGINING

Katalin Karikó, PhD, a Hungarian-born biochemist, first laid the foundation for the messenger RNA (mRNA) therapeutics that have been used to develop the COVID-19 vaccine (Garde and Saltzman 2020). Messenger RNA transfers the information from DNA to ribosomes to make specific proteins in cells. Karikó hypothesized that if a genetically coded synthetic mRNA was injected into mice, the cells in the body would make the specific protein instructed by the synthetic mRNA. In the 1990s, when she was faculty at the University of Pennsylvania, Karikó submitted several grant proposals on this idea. The proposals were repeatedly rejected, as the reviewers thought this concept would not work because of the potential degradation of the synthetic mRNA in the body and the potentially dangerous inflammatory immune reaction.

Despite professional setbacks, Karikó believed in her idea and continued the work with little financial support. Karikó began collaborating with immunologist/mRNA vaccine researcher Drew Weissman, MD; together they came up with the idea to modify the structure of uridine, one of the four nucleosides of the building blocks of RNA. As they predicted, the modified mRNA encapsulated in a lipid nanoparticle was taken up by cells; Karikó and Weissman then extended this technology to deliver the synthetic mRNA in mice.

They published a paper in 2005 (Karikó et al. 2005) and obtained NIH funding, and this new technology was patented by the University of Pennsylvania. BioNTech, a German company known for developing vaccines, licensed this technology, as did Moderna, a biotech company in Boston.

Karikó is now the senior vice president of BioNTech RNA Pharmaceuticals. The Pfizer-BioNTech partnership developed an mRNA vaccine designed to induce neutralizing antibodies against a portion of the SARS-CoV-2 "spike" protein that the virus uses to gain access into human cells. The antibodies against the "spike" protein recognize and neutralize SARS-CoV-2, thus preventing the infection.

Although Karikó encountered early setbacks in her research, she never gave up and always "imagined how the synthetic mRNA approach could treat so many diseases."

REIMAGINING A WORK-LIFE BALANCE

Ideally, having a good work-life balance would give one satisfaction, fulfillment, a sense of purpose, and empathy. Early during the pandemic, a barrier to optimal work-life balance existed for parents (more often mothers), particularly single parents, as they juggled work with childcare and home schooling.

People in the workforce are on different trajectories. Some just starting, some climbing up and trying to reach cruising altitude, some pushing the "reset" button, and some pushing the "rest" button. All too often, people (myself included) are too carried away in their work and give little attention to their life outside of work. Organizations conduct workshops to teach us ways to restructure our lives, which may not seem like rocket science, but it may be nearly as difficult. In what ways can we strike a good work-life balance? I leave this to the experts to ponder. If we take the time to pause and contemplate it, we will be off to a great start.

REIMAGINING RELATIONSHIPS

Professional advice on improving relationships is available everywhere—in workshops, talk shows, magazine articles. This is all well and good and may work for some people, but often we just need to reimagine the little things that are forgotten. Yes, I understand, "Physician, heal thyself," and I think it goes well with "better late than never." In his article, *10 Ways To Reimagine Your Relationship*, Barton Goldsmith, PhD, says "Doing new things together, and old things in new ways, makes your love stronger." He proposes several ideas to reimagine relationships:

Let go of the past. Learn to forgive and forget and focus on the positives. Be grateful for each other and treat each day as a blessing. Write down at least one thing (daily or weekly) that you appreciate about your partner.

Create your fantasy vacation. Daydreaming about your ideal vacation can be fun! During the pandemic, this may be hard to fathom, but things will get back to normal. And when you are able to take a vacation, you will be ready.

Take a class together. Or do other activities with your partner: Take a virtual cooking class, learn CPR, learn a new language, take a walk through the park.

Have lunch together once a week. This will help break the monotony.

Ask your partner twenty questions. Show curiosity in your partner's interests. What are some things you've always wanted to know about your partner but never took the time to ask?

To this list, I'll add: Never be afraid to poke fun of yourself. Self-deprecating humor can ease those tense moments.

REIMAGINING STRESS REDUCTION THROUGH MINDFULNESS

Emerging science convincingly shows that routine exercise, yoga, meditation, and mindful meditation can alleviate stress, anxiety, and depression. Herbert Benson, MD (Benson-Henry Institute for Mind Body Medicine at Massachusetts General Hospital), pioneered the beneficial effects of meditation (e.g., lowering blood pressure and heart rate, and increasing brain activity). Functional MRI studies support the beneficial aspects of meditation to combat depression and anxiety.

Suzanne Westbrook, MD, a retired doctor of internal medicine, says, "Our mind wanders all the time, either reviewing the past or planning for the future" (Mineo 2018). Mindfulness teaches the skill of paying attention to the present, and that life is in the moment. Mindfulness is not about trying to empty the mind; rather, it is about remaining present. It is a practice designed to improve brain health. Taking a slow deep breath through the nostrils (i.e., inhaling) and then slowly breathing out through the mouth (i.e., exhaling) will help you relax, reenergize, and reconnect. Repeat this breathing technique about ten times. Use it as a "balance break" as needed during tense times (e.g., grant preparation). Mindfulness will improve your focus on the task at hand and your ability to face challenges with a healthy attitude, reduced stress, and increased energy. Mindfulness could be incorporated into many things—eating, conversation, listening. Some people practice twenty to thirty minutes of meditation that involves "mindful body scan," during which one notices the sensations one is feeling without judgement. Indeed, mindfulness is presently at the top of the wellness universe as a stress reduction technique!

LONG COVID (OR LONG-HAULER SYNDROME) AND SIDE EFFECTS OF THE PANDEMIC

I wrote a review on how oxidative stress and inflammation contribute to the severity of COVID-19 (Kalyanaraman 2021b). The following is an excerpt from the article:

> The common symptoms of COVID-19 are fever or chills, shortness of breath, fatigue, muscle or body aches,

headache, dry cough, loss of taste and smell, sore throat, congestion or runny nose, nausea or vomiting, and diarrhea. Individuals experiencing long COVID, or long-haulers, are increasing in numbers. Nearly 10% of surviving COVID-19 patients experience cardiovascular or neurological complications. It is critically important to develop therapies for persistent symptoms (memory fog, loss of smell, and digestive and heart problems) and to reduce cardiovascular inflammation in long COVID patients. Prophylactic treatment may include supplementation with N-acetylcysteine, GSH, CuraMed (a curcumin supplement), and omega-3. Mitochondrial drugs (e.g., metformin, honokiol, Mito-Q, Mito-magnolol, Mito-apocynin) have been shown to inhibit immunosuppressive cells and inflammation (Langley et al. 2017). Because these drugs are relatively nontoxic and do not suppress the immune system like the conventional steroidal drugs, they may be used prophylactically in a preventative setting. Clearly, using mitochondria-targeted drugs and other known immune boosters to enhance mitochondrial fitness and the immune system of host cells infected with SARS-CoV-2 (Burtscher et al. 2020) may provide protection against or lessen the severity of COVID-19 (Burtscher et al. 2020). Female COVID-19 patients, as compared with male COVID-19 patients, elicit much higher T cell activation (Takahashi et al. 2020). Male COVID-19 patients have higher plasma levels of innate immune cytokines (e.g., IL-8) (Takahashi et al. 2020). Drugs selectively enhancing mitochondrial biogenesis (resveratrol, quercetin) and mitochondrial function should be tested in clinical trials for COVID-19 treatment. Honokiol, an active anti-inflammatory component extracted from the bark of the *Magnolia officinalis* has been shown to improve mitochondrial function via activation of sirtuin 3 (Pillai et al. 2017).

> Phytotherapy with plant-derived polyphenolics was suggested as a plausible method to mitigate SARS-CoV-2-induced oxidative stress and inflammation (Levy et al. 2020).

After a little more than two years, the number of COVID-19 deaths in the United States reached nearly a million. The United States has one of the most advanced healthcare systems in the world, yet ranks third or fourth in the world with respect to the number of COVID-19 deaths.

Two years into the pandemic, the focus turned to unvaccinated people who were not infected with the virus or who were infected but had relatively minor reactions. Is it because of their enhanced immunity? How can each of us improve our immune system and its ability to fight pathogens? This depends on various factors and lifestyle modifications. How can we enhance antiviral immunity through lifestyle modifications? There are no prescriptions for this. Experts agree on the following: exercise regularly, eat nutritious meals, get adequate sleep, reduce stress through work-life balance, and adapt a positive growth mindset that includes gratitude, humility, creativity, and living in the moment. Of course, sugar, salt, and alcohol should be consumed only in moderation.

Following are my suggestions for boosting one's immune system through lifestyle modifications: Exercise three to four times per week, each time about forty minutes. Include a twenty-minute cardiovascular workout (stationary biking, treadmill, or running indoors or outdoors depending on the weather). Alternate between cardio and isometric or resistance training for twenty minutes. Alternate between biceps, triceps, shoulders, back, chest, legs, and stretching. The key when exercising regularly is to concentrate on the muscle you are working on, along with proper breathing, another very important component. Fitness centers have a wide variety of machines, and for people over sixty, it is better to avoid free weights and use resistance training. Of course, always make sure you are sufficiently hydrated.

As much as possible, all of us—but especially anyone who has underlying disease or is immunocompromised—should pay attention to what we eat. Emerging research suggests that maintaining gut health through increased intake of fiber, fruits, vegetables, nuts, whole grains, legumes, and low-fat dairy products is important for controlling inflammatory diseases, not only in the gut but in remote organs like the brain, through the so-called "gut-brain axis." Minimizing or eliminating consumption of fried, refined, and high-fat foods, and substituting with baked foods, whole-grain foods, and lean meats might decrease gut inflammation and enhance beneficial immune cells.

Initially, these regimented approaches may be difficult to follow and maintain, but they will get easier with time and practice. Everything in moderation including moderation is another way to ease into this mindset.

One big question looms: Is it possible to prevent future pandemics? A recent report suggests that transformative actions should be undertaken on health and biodiversity (Vora et al. 2022). Mitigation or prevention of spillover events that trigger the transfer of pathogens from animals into people was suggested through implementing actions to decrease human-induced environmental changes such as deforestation, eliminating the trade of live wild animals in commercial markets, enhancing the biosecurity of farmed animals, monitoring and improving the health of immunosuppressed people in hot spots, and increasing global funding for pandemics research. Failure to adopt such mitigative measures is predicted to significantly increase the annual probability of global pandemics in the coming years.

EPILOGUE

"The secret of getting started is getting started."
—Mark Twain

The secret to completing a project is to get started. My journey up to this point—from Bombay to El Paso to Tuscaloosa to Chapel "Thrill" to Brew City in the Cheese State—has been a long and winding, and exhilarating ride. Looking back, I would do it all over again. I am endlessly grateful to my parents, wife, children, granddaughter, family, relatives, and friends in India, in the United States, and from around the world.

I would like to share a few takeaways and life lessons from this journey with aspiring young foreign and local students, budding scientists, professionals, and anyone who strives to achieve success in their endeavors. Always remember the positive things you have accomplished, no matter how small or big, at every stage of your life. This can be applied to everything you do going forward! It is all about mindset. The mindset *I have done this before, and I can do it again* is key to achieving progress. If you keep focusing on the positive things you have accomplished, you will develop the mindset of growth. This growth mindset is the foundation on which you'll build your career. Now, what is mindset? It is a set of attitudes and beliefs that we each hold and cultivate; and are essential in determining our achievements and success.

I was asked to deliver the 2022 MCW Graduate School Hooding Ceremony Address to graduates, advisors, friends, and family. I watched countless YouTube motivational speeches delivered by famous people to college graduates. Many of them were great, but I could not relate to their stories. Then I came across an inspiring graduation speech at Yale University by Shah Rukh Khan, a famous Indian Bollywood actor. He spoke about success and failures in his life, and pointed out that we live in a world focused on success. I was so moved by his speech that I incorporated some of his ideas into my Hooding Ceremony speech: Success is a wonderful thing; one should enjoy it and take credit for it. But success does not exist without failure. Some people try to model their lives after other successful people, but success is not transferable, and it does not provide wisdom. The true path to success is overcoming the fear of failure.

Everyone will experience failure at some point in our lives. As we all know, failure is not a pleasant experience. It is the response to failure that matters. If one approach does not work, try another. When you fail, take note of what went wrong and learn from it. If you find you are experiencing repeated failures, it is important to pause and reevaluate the strategy. Consider Thomas Edison, who perfected the light bulb after ten thousand attempts. Of course, Edison viewed his failures with a positive spin, and said that he discovered ten thousand ways how *not* to do this experiment. That is a remarkable mindset worthy of emulation.

As Kahn said, "Failure is an amazing teacher." The lessons we learn from failures are invaluable. When we have a growth mindset, we will be better equipped to handle failures, and find a formula for turning them into successes. Success can be viewed as the difference between what we are able to do, and what we actually do; shortening this gap will help overcome failure.

I believe success is a combination of passion, commitment, and the ability to learn from failure. What else is needed for a successful career? This is where other factors—such as humility, gratitude, creativity, and empathy—come into play, and our mindset begins to expand.

Remember that each of us is a work in progress, and we must continuously expand our mindset. New research shows that gratitude works to improve mental health. People who consciously "count their blessings" tend to be happier and less depressed.

Empathy is another trait that empowers mindset. It is the ability to sense and share the feelings of another. In the words of Satya Nadella, chair and CEO of Microsoft, empathy is "the ability to be able to put ourselves in other people's shoes and see the world as they see it." In his book *Hit Refresh*, he wrote, "Ideas excite me. Empathy grounds and centers me." Simon Baron-Cohen, clinical psychologist from the University of Cambridge, United Kingdom, wrote, "Empathy is like a universal solvent. Any problem immersed in empathy becomes soluble."

As we progress in life, and in our careers, one thing that will remain constant is change: people change, we change, the world changes—we've all seen this firsthand—and our dreams and passions change. When we experience change, having a growth mindset will help us adapt.

Now, a few more parting words of wisdom from my life experience: Think for yourself. Be creative. Expand your knowledge. Exchange ideas. No matter what you do, embrace new and innovative approaches to solve problems. As Albert Einstein said, "We cannot solve our problems with the same thinking we used when we created them."

The most important currency we have is integrity, and there are no shortcuts in science or in any other profession.

Finally, social connection and human interaction are vital for prolonged mental fitness and well-being. Matthew Lieberman said in his book *Social: Why Our Brains Are Wired to Connect* that "social adaptations are central to making us the most successful species on earth." Going forward, one of the biggest challenges we may all face is how we avoid or replace the despair and darkness that sometimes creep in, with hope and enlightenment. Interacting and connecting with others will open lines of communication and light up regions of sadness and depression in the brain like a Christmas tree, the same way listening to the music you love does!

The significance of human connection has been realized by famous poets from all over the world. Below is an excerpt from a poem by Nobel Laureate Sir Rabindranath Tagore (1861–1941), who also composed the National Anthem of India. Tagore received the Nobel Prize in Literature in 1913; he was the first Indian citizen and first Asian to be awarded the Nobel Prize.

> Alone I can 'Say' but together we can 'Talk'
> Alone I can 'Enjoy' but together we can 'Celebrate'
> Alone I can 'Smile' but together we can 'Laugh'

That's the beauty of human relations. We are nothing without each other. So, stay connected!

ACKNOWLEDGMENTS

I would like to express my gratitude and thanks to my parents, grandmother, uncles, and aunts who are all in heaven, and to my brother, sister, and cousins—Kumar, Sarada, Srinivasan, Tharakam, Sushila, Sakuntala, Kalpakam, Mangalam, and Bhavani—for the care and support they provided when I was in Madras and Bombay. Sadly, Sushila passed away recently. To Ramani, my brother-in-law and Sarada's husband, who passed away a few years ago; to Jaya, my brother's wife, and Uma, Srinivasan's wife, and Seetha.

My sincere gratitude to all my friends who supported, encouraged, mentored, or inspired me along my journey. In Madras: Kumar, Shankar, Murali, Gopal, Sunda, and their spouses; sadly, Chandru and Jaggu passed away. In El Paso: Ragu, Rao, and Keith. In Tuscaloosa: Lowell, Jerry, Bill, Ben, Richard, and the late Dale. In Chapel Hill: Ron, Mary, Birandra, Earl, Bob, Mike, and others. At MCW: Roger, Jim, Chris, Pete, Deb, Ming, Mike, Carol, Daisy, Ravi, Ivor, and many other collaborators; my graduate students; my postdoctoral fellows; the Biophysics faculty; and the Biophysics staff and administration—Chris, Kristin, Marian, Jane, Lydia, and Linda. My collaborators: Tad,

Victor, Bruce, Joe, Henry, Rafael, Murali, Kupps, Narayan, Navdeep, and Anumantha.

A special heartfelt thank you to my wife, Lilian; my daughter, Regina; my son, Rajiv; my son-in-law, Scott; and my granddaughter, Marley.

To my nieces and nephews, Jayashree, Sarathy and sons; Babu, Uma and sons; and Asha, Prasad and sons.

To my in-laws, the late Carlos and Elisa; Lilian's sisters, Elisa, Silvia, and Maria (Wichi); my brother-in-law, Gaines, who motivated me to write this book; my late brother-in-law, Jon; and to our nieces Michelle, Sheri, Maylea, Juliana and their families.

To our friends Roland, Steve, Zimmy, Dave, Jim and Mary, and to a host of others in Milwaukee.

To our Elmhurst village friends, Sue, Hungsun, and family; Anne, Dan, and family; Jillie Bean; Lore; the late Willie, Otto, and Paula; Jeannette, Cameron and family; Sara, Miguel, and family; and Juan, Carmen, and family.

Writing this book has been both challenging and rewarding. I would like to express my deepest appreciation to Jane, Lydia, and Lilian for editing, revising, providing constructive comments on, and helping bring this memoir to life, and to Regina for her original art on the cover.

To all of you who have provided support, collegiality, and friendship to me along my journey from Bombay to Brew City, I'm profoundly grateful.

BIBLIOGRAPHY

Baas, Jeroen, Kevin Boyack, and John P.A. Ioannidis. 2021. August 2021 data-update for "Updated science-wide author databases of standardized citation indicators". Mendeley Data. Version 3: 19 Oct 2021.

Burtscher, J., G. Cappellano, A. Omori, T. Koshiba, and G. P. Millet. 2020. "Mitochondria: In the Cross Fire of SARS-CoV-2 and Immunity." iScience 23 (10):101631. doi: 10.1016/j.isci.2020.101631.

Card, D., and G. B. Dahl. 2011. "Family violence and football: the effect of unexpected emotional cues on violent behavior." Q J Econ 126 (1):103-43. doi: 10.1093/qje/qjr001.

Centers for Disease Control and Prevention. 2021. "Parasites - Guinea Worm." https://www.cdc.gov/parasites/guineaworm/.

Forbes. 2022. "Profile: Mukesh Ambani." accessed February 21, 2022. https://www.forbes.com/profile/mukesh-ambani/?sh=5115d367214c.

Garde, Damian, and Jonathan Saltzman. 2020. "The story of mRNA: How a once-dismissed idea became a leading technology in the Covid vaccine race." STAT.

Health Facts. 2018. "What is the longest tapeworm ever removed from a person?". https://healthfacts.blog/2018/01/19/what-is-the-longest-tapeworm-ever-removed-from-a-person/.

Kalyanaraman, B. 2020a. Every Virus Needs a Host and the Answer Lies Within Each of Us. *Transformational Times.*

Kalyanaraman, B. 2020b. The Tuskegee Study: Overcoming Racial Disparities in Vaccinations and Rebuilding the Trust of Black Americans. *Transformational Times.*

Kalyanaraman, B. 2021a. Reimagine, it's Easy if You Try. *Transformational Times.*

Kalyanaraman, B. 2021b. "Reactive oxygen species, proinflammatory and immunosuppressive mediators induced in COVID-19: overlapping biology with cancer." *RSC Chem Biol* 2 (5):1402-1414. doi: 10.1039/d1cb00042j.

Karikó, K., M. Buckstein, H. Ni, and D. Weissman. 2005. "Suppression of RNA recognition by Toll-like receptors: the impact of nucleoside modification and the evolutionary origin of RNA." *Immunity* 23 (2):165-75. doi: 10.1016/j.immuni.2005.06.008.

Langley, M., A. Ghosh, A. Charli, S. Sarkar, M. Ay, J. Luo, J. Zielonka, T. Brenza, B. Bennett, H. Jin, S. Ghaisas, B. Schlichtmann, D. Kim, V. Anantharam, A. Kanthasamy, B. Narasimhan, B. Kalyanaraman, and A. G. Kanthasamy.

2017. "Mito-Apocynin Prevents Mitochondrial Dysfunction, Microglial Activation, Oxidative Damage, and Progressive Neurodegeneration in MitoPark Transgenic Mice." *Antioxid Redox Signal* 27 (14):1048-1066. doi: 10.1089/ars.2016.6905.

Lessons In Leadership Institute. 2018. *Nick Saban and The Process: Applying the Principles that Drive the Greatest College Football Coach in History to Your Life (Lessons in Leadership)*: Independently Published.

Levy, E., E. Delvin, V. Marcil, and S. Spahis. 2020. "Can phytotherapy with polyphenols serve as a powerful approach for the prevention and therapy tool of novel coronavirus disease 2019 (COVID-19)?" *Am J Physiol Endocrinol Metab* 319 (4):E689-e708. doi: 10.1152/ajpendo.00298.2020.

Lewsing, K. 2022. "Apple becomes first U.S. company to reach $3 trillion market cap." CNBC LLC. https://www.cnbc.com/2022/01/03/apple-becomes-first-us-company-to-reach-3-trillion-market-cap.html.

McConnell, Brighton. 2020. "'He Changed the Look of Franklin Street': Mickey Ewell Remembered for His Restaurants, Relationships." *97.9 The Hill and Chapelboro.com.*

Mineo, Liz. 2018. "With mindfulness, life's in the moment." *The Harvard Gazettte*. https://news.harvard.edu/gazette/story/2018/04/less-stress-clearer-thoughts-with-mindfulness-meditation/.

Moore, Karl. 2011. "The Best Way To Innovation? - An Important Lesson from India." https://www.forbes.com/

sites/karlmoore/2011/05/24/the-best-way-to-innovation-an-important-lesson-from-india/?sh=307e8c962861.

Mumbai Dabbawala. "About Us." https://mumbaidabbawala.in/about-us/.

Myers, Marc. 2015. "How Steely Dan Created 'Deacon Blues'." https://www.wsj.com/articles/how-steely-dan-created-deacon-blues-1441727645.

Philips, Cyriac A., and Amrish Sahney. 2017. "Taenia solium." *New England Journal of Medicine* 376 (4):e4. doi: 10.1056/NEJMicm1606747.

Pillai, V. B., A. Kanwal, Y. H. Fang, W. W. Sharp, S. Samant, J. Arbiser, and M. P. Gupta. 2017. "Honokiol, an activator of Sirtuin-3 (SIRT3) preserves mitochondria and protects the heart from doxorubicin-induced cardiomyopathy in mice." *Oncotarget* 8 (21):34082-34098. doi: 10.18632/oncotarget.16133.

Sankari, Rathina. 2021. "Mumbai's Dabbawalas Delivered Thousands of Lunches A Day— Lockdown Changed Everything." Last Modified August 17, 2021. https://food52.com/blog/26484-mumbai-dabbawalas-pivot-during-coronavirus.

Sengar, Resham. 2018. "Travel Lesson - The Story of Mubai's Dabbawalas." https://timesofindia.indiatimes.com/travel/eating-out/travel-lesson-the-story-of-mumbais-dabbawalas/as66882538.cms.

Takahashi, T., M. K. Ellingson, P. Wong, B. Israelow, C. Lucas, J. Klein, J. Silva, T. Mao, J. E. Oh, M. Tokuyama, P. Lu, A. Venkataraman, A. Park, F. Liu, A. Meir, J. Sun, E. Y. Wang,

A. Casanovas-Massana, A. L. Wyllie, C. B. F. Vogels, R. Earnest, S. Lapidus, I. M. Ott, A. J. Moore, A. Shaw, J. B. Fournier, C. D. Odio, S. Farhadian, C. Dela Cruz, N. D. Grubaugh, W. L. Schulz, A. M. Ring, A. I. Ko, S. B. Omer, and A. Iwasaki. 2020. "Sex differences in immune responses that underlie COVID-19 disease outcomes." *Nature* 588 (7837):315-320. doi: 10.1038/s41586-020-2700-3.

Vora, N. M., L. Hannah, S. Lieberman, M. M. Vale, R. K. Plowright, and A. S. Bernstein. 2022. "Want to prevent pandemics? Stop spillovers." *Nature* 605 (7910):419-422. doi: 10.1038/d41586-022-01312-y.

World Health Organization. 2022. "Dracunculiasis (guinea-worm disease)." https://www.who.int/news-room/fact-sheets/detail/dracunculiasis-(guinea-worm-disease).

World Population Review. "Mumbai Population 2022." https://worldpopulationreview.com/world-cities/mumbai-population.

ABOUT THE AUTHOR

Balaraman "Raman" Kalyanaraman, PhD, lives in Wauwatosa, Wisconsin, with his wife, Lilian. He is father to Regina and Rajiv, father-in-law to Scott, and grandfather to Marley. Raman received his Bachelor of Science degree in Chemistry from Loyola College, University of Madras (Chennai, India), his Master of Science degree in Chemistry from the Indian Institute of Technology (Bombay, India), and his PhD in Chemistry from the University of Alabama (Tuscaloosa). He was a visiting fellow in the Laboratory of Environmental Biophysics, National Institute of Environmental Health Sciences (Research Triangle Park, North Carolina).

Raman joined the Medical College of Wisconsin (MCW) in 1981 as a research associate (postdoctoral fellow). He rose through the ranks of MCW to become the Harry R. and Angeline

E. Quadracci Professor in Parkinson's Research and chair (2003–2022) of the Department of Biophysics.

He has authored more than 400 research articles and over sixty reviews and book chapters, which earned him a place on Stanford University's list of the top one percent most-cited scientists in the world in the fields of biochemistry and molecular biology, oncology and carcinogenesis, and biomedical research.

Raman is an authority on the fundamental biochemistry of free radicals, and has developed novel approaches that have contributed to the growth and development of this scientific field.

He has applied these methods to advance the understanding of the role of mitochondria in cancer, Parkinson's disease, cardiac injury, neuronal injury, and vascular biology. Raman's research contributions have been recognized with numerous awards, including the Silver Medal for Biology and Medicine from the International Electron Paramagnetic Resonance Society; the Lifetime Achievement Award from the Society for Free Radical Biology and Medicine; and MCW's Distinguished Service Award, in tribute to his significant and distinguished service to MCW. More than fifty research scientists, postdoctoral fellows, graduate students, and undergraduate students have benefitted from his mentorship, as have hundreds of graduate and medical students from his teaching activities.

www.ingramcontent.com/pod-product-compliance
Lightning Source LLC
Chambersburg PA
CBHW041752010726
47507CB00009B/371

* 9 7 8 1 6 4 5 3 8 4 9 7 7 *